D0948187

# MASTERING THE ART OF RECRUITING

# MASTERING THE ART OF RECRUITING

## How to Hire the Right Candidate for the Job

Michael Travis

 PRAEGER

AN IMPRINT OF ABC-CLIO, LLC
Santa Barbara, California • Denver, Colorado • Oxford, England

**Library of Congress Cataloging-in-Publication Data**

Travis, Michael, 1962-
   Mastering the art of recruiting : how to hire the right candidate for the job / Michael Travis.
      pages cm
   Includes bibliographical references and index.
   ISBN 978-1-4408-3144-7 (print : alk. paper) — ISBN 978-1-4408-3145-4 (e-book)
1. Employees—Recruiting. 2. Employee selection. 3. Personnel management.   I. Title.
HF5549.5.R44T73 2015
658.3'111—dc23          2014028324

ISBN: 978-1-4408-3144-7
EISBN: 978-1-4408-3145-4

19   18   17   16   15      1   2   3   4   5

This book is also available on the World Wide Web as an eBook.
Visit www.abc-clio.com for details.

Praeger
An Imprint of ABC-CLIO, LLC

ABC-CLIO, LLC
130 Cremona Drive, P.O. Box 1911
Santa Barbara, California 93116-1911

This book is printed on acid-free paper ∞

Manufactured in the United States of America

*For my father, John Travis*

# Contents

# Chapter 1

# The Messy Business of Assessing People

Great-Aunt Colette left her life as a snake charmer with Ringling Brothers to become a fortune-teller on the boardwalk in Atlantic City. Dressed in a flowing robe and a turban, she peered into a crystal ball and saw the future.

I didn't inherit any of my aunt's soothsaying ability, if she had any, but I am confident making this prediction:

*Finding great people is your number-one business problem.*

That may seem like a bold statement since I know nothing about you or your company, but it's a safe bet. All of us who've spent time in the corporate world know that acquiring and keeping talent is the number-one problem for every business. No matter what industry you're in or where you sit in the organization, identifying, recruiting, and retaining the very best people is your top priority. More than any other factor, talent is the key to exceptional performance.

Companies that have mastered the acquisition of talent enjoy a huge advantage. Their superior people design more innovative products, manufacture with higher quality, sell and market more effectively, and generally run circles around their competitors.

*Mastering the Art of Recruiting* is for executives who want to take their hiring performance to the next level. It will also be of interest to savvy up-and-coming managers who understand that hiring great people will speed their advancement to the executive level. If you are committed to improving the quality of your hires, this book will help you, and if you apply the principles in this book consistently over time, you will put yourself on the fast track to becoming a recruiting master.

This book is more than just a tool for your own professional development. If you put it into the hands of the managers in your group, it will help improve hiring throughout your entire organization.

## The Heavy Price of Bad Hires

It will come as no surprise that most companies fail to achieve passing grades when it comes to recruiting. One study showed that 40 percent of new hires fail within eighteen months, and other estimates are even higher.[1]

This dismal state of affairs exacts a very high price. Direct costs of a bad hire (recruiting fees, relocation, training, severance, and more) can total two or three times the new hire's annual salary, but those aren't the only losses. Indirect costs, such as lost opportunity and lost productivity due to disruption of the organization, while harder to quantify, can easily be several times direct costs. Bad hires, especially at the executive level, are a financial disaster.

What about the cost to executives who repeatedly make bad hires? Quite simply, the inability to build a great team can end a career, or at least leave it stuck in neutral. Executives who want to advance must master the fundamental skill of recognizing and attracting top people.

Given the critical importance of recruiting and the epidemic of bad hires, it would be natural to assume that companies are working hard to improve the hiring skills of their employees. Surprisingly, that's not the case. Most companies provide little to no education on recruiting for their young hiring managers, and when they do it's often narrowly focused on employment law and human resources policies instead of how to make the right selection. Utterly unprepared, new managers are thrown into the deep end of the pool and expected to swim.

My experience was fairly typical. As an inexperienced manager at a small high-tech company, I knew nothing about hiring, and like many ambitious young people I had no idea how ignorant I was. My employer, like most, didn't see the need to teach the basics of recruiting. What little instruction we received was about HR policies.

So when it came time to make my first hire, I forged ahead blindly. Everyone else in the company seemed to think I should know how to do this stuff, so I didn't ask for help, though I desperately needed it. I ended up with a marginal hire. That was better than I deserved, given my poor hiring skills and the shoddy process I had run, but much less than I needed.

Notably, the human resources director who was allegedly supporting me did very little to help. She assisted with the administrative aspects of the hire, but gave no direction on interviewing, references, or any of the other steps that are important to selecting the right candidate. In hindsight, it's clear she didn't provide that help because she couldn't. She was inexperienced herself, and like many in HR management she was drowning in administrative minutiae and out of touch with the things that mattered to the business.

How bad can it get? Here's an example that's amusing because it is so extreme. A friend related a story that happened in his workplace. (As with all anecdotes in this book in which companies are not identified, details have been changed to make the businesses and individuals unidentifiable. In other words, if you think you recognize someone, you're wrong.)

A young biotech company with a promising new technology needed to hire a new head of regulatory affairs. Regulatory affairs is a mission-critical function in life sciences companies because it defines the strategy for winning regulatory approval and manages relations with the Food and Drug Administration (FDA).

The CEO identified a candidate who was aggressive and very smart. They hit it off right away, and thereafter nothing could deter the CEO from proceeding with the hire at full speed, despite the vice president of human resource's protestations that something wasn't right. After a cursory reference check, the CEO extended an offer, and the new vice president joined the company.

It wasn't long before trouble started. The new executive screamed at his staff. When traveling, he was always accompanied by his female assistant, who appeared to be helping in ways that violated company policy. The company should have dismissed him immediately, but despite the obvious dysfunction they kept him on.

Surely they regretted their inaction later, when (largely due to the failed vice president's mismanagement) the FDA rejected the company's application to market its drug. Over a period of years, the firm withered away, suffering the corporate equivalent of the death penalty. The CEO who made the hire was fired, and his career never recovered from the high-profile failure.

That's a hiring nightmare worthy of a soap opera, but most bad hires are not nearly so dramatic. The typical bad hire is no more than adequate. He is competent but does not have the imagination, energy, or leadership ability to take the organization anywhere new. He is mediocre.

In contrast, a great hire can transform a business. Here's another story, this time from my own client work.

A technology company recruited a new vice president of manufacturing to replace a beloved, longtime incumbent who had recently retired. It was a delicate situation for the new VP, because many in the department worried that a new leader would bring dramatic and unwelcome changes.

Looking at the organization with fresh eyes, the new executive immediately saw opportunities to make operations much more efficient. Implementing the changes, however, would be challenging. There was a high risk of creating disruption that would be counterproductive, and the rank and file feared that efficiency would mean layoffs.

The new VP proved to be a masterful leader. She involved her team, securing their enthusiastic support, and found a way to make changes without demoralizing job cuts. Her capable leadership saved the company millions in her first year alone, and the savings were invested in strategic initiatives that grew the company's revenue and market share for years afterward. She added value to the business that was orders of magnitude greater than her generous compensation. Naturally, her outstanding results put her career on an even faster track than it had been on before.

Her boss was elated, of course, because she helped him deliver outstanding results for the business. The vice president of manufacturing was his first major hire, and he'd been under intense pressure to make it a success. Her stellar performance put his career in the fast lane, too.

As an executive, your success depends on hiring great people. Just as the manager of a baseball team can't win games without talented players, a business leader can't succeed without the right people on his or her staff. Regardless of your other talents, the trajectory of your career will be determined by your ability to attract the best players to work for you. Our generation's business legends—Jack Welch and Alan Mulally, to name just two—are renowned for their ability to identify, attract, and develop great people.

Be honest—how good is your track record? Have you hired your share of top performers, or have you made some poor choices? Have you been frustrated by your inability to identify or attract the people you need? Chances are, if you're reading this book, you think you could do better, and you are right. Making good hiring decisions is hard, and no one gets it right all the time. No matter how good you are today, you'll find room for improvement.

## Hiring: Art or Science?

Recruiting great people is challenging. There are dozens of books on hiring, each with a unique take on the subject from a self-described expert. Many of these books urge readers to abandon the use of intuition or "gut feel" in hiring, and to adopt the author's system for "scientific" hiring. One author touts his "silver bullet assessment technique." Indeed, there's a very good market in selling the illusion of scientific hiring. Just ask the hundreds of vendors of assessment tests.

The rise of data analytics in human resources has made the illusion of scientific hiring even more compelling. Certainly it would be more efficient if businesses could emulate Billy Beane, the general manager of the Oakland A's featured in Michael Lewis's book *Moneyball*, and choose talent based on numbers and percentages. If we ever got to a point where a person's performance could be summarized in an Excel spreadsheet, we could dispense with interviews altogether!

If only it were so simple. It's natural to wish there were a way to cut through all those messy human factors and get to hard facts. If there were a "scientific" way to hire, we could objectively measure the relevant aspects of candidates' personalities, skills, and other qualities, make perfect decisions every time, and brag about our 100 percent success rate. But of course, that's not happening. We need only look at results from the real world to determine that "scientific hiring" is a charade.

Ultimately, the appeal of so-called scientific hiring systems is that they promise a shortcut through the complex and difficult business of assessing people. There's a natural human tendency to look for an easy way out, as demonstrated by the continual onslaught of advertising for "effortless" weight loss or get-rich-quick schemes. Against all the evidence, people keep buying those products. You don't have to be so gullible. Don't waste time and effort looking for scientific assessment tools, foolproof hiring systems, and other gimmicks. There are no shortcuts to learning the skills and techniques that make up the art of hiring.

Hiring is challenging because it requires us to make decisions based on human qualities that are impossible to quantify. People simply can't be measured in the way we measure revenue or gross margin. Hiring forces us to rely on "soft" people skills that aren't taught in school, and that makes many executives uncomfortable. That's why I purposefully chose to use the word *Art* in the title of this book.

Think about great hiring managers you know, the ones who stand out for their ability to recognize and recruit top talent. They can often tell in just minutes whether a candidate will be a good fit for their organization. Their feel for people looks mysterious to those who don't have it. Is it an inborn trait? If so, there's no hope of becoming an expert at hiring without it. You either have it or you don't.

Happily for all of us, that's not the case. The intuitive feel for people that looks so mysterious is a learnable skill. Anyone can acquire it with hard work, because it is the by-product of expertise. I know from experience, because I've been through the learning process myself.

Malcolm Gladwell, noted author of the bestseller *Blink: The Power of Thinking Without Thinking*, describes the kind of intuition I'm talking about. Gladwell explains that experts can make highly accurate snap decisions, a skill he calls *rapid cognition*.[2] The key to this skill is expertise. Experts know which data is important and which is extraneous, and that enables them to dramatically simplify complex problems. They have become so good at what they do that they can make difficult decisions and judgments in their unconscious minds. To the outsider, and sometimes even to the experts themselves, answers seem to pop out of nowhere, as if by magic.

There's a risk to relying on intuition, so it must be used with great care. If you're not an expert, quick decisions are a roll of the dice, and the results can be disastrous. Snap decisions that don't have a foundation in expertise are usually bad decisions. If you're new to hiring, or if you have a track record that needs improvement, relying on your gut can lead to serious mistakes.

## The Process

Right about now you may be thinking, "Great, I need years of experience to become an expert, but I don't have years. I need to improve now."

It's true that developing expertise takes years of practice, but there is good news. You don't have to become an expert to dramatically improve. Anyone can improve his or her hiring performance right away through disciplined adherence to a sound recruiting process. And with time, consistently following a good process develops expertise, just as regular practice builds any other skill.

There's a saying that "perfect practice makes perfect." I had a music teacher who used to tell me, "Slow down to a speed where you can play it right. If you're making too many mistakes, you're just training yourself to do it the wrong way." Applied to hiring, the lesson is that if you consistently use good hiring practices, you'll learn to do things correctly and acquire expertise faster. Conversely, if you don't follow good processes, you'll make a lot of mistakes and learn slowly.

Whether you're a hiring novice or an expert, process is essential. It's a road map that helps you cover all the bases in a way that results in high-quality decisions. From defining the job to closing a deal, success depends on the disciplined execution of countless small tasks. Details matter, and process helps you make sure you don't miss important steps.

It's important to emphasize that experts can't throw away the process. In fact, expertise is defined, in part, by the ability to execute the process with great skill. Consider the great cellist Yo-Yo Ma, who's undoubtedly expert at his art. Does expertise mean he can take liberties with the notes in a piece of music? Of course not. He is an expert because he can play those notes with great creativity and insight.

What are these good hiring practices? That's the focus of this book, which provides a detailed, step-by-step guide to sound hiring process. Along the way, it identifies the most common points where hiring managers make mistakes, and explains how you can avoid them.

The process described in this book comprises six steps, and is the same one I use in my own executive search practice. It's been refined through nearly two decades of experience recruiting senior executives and my work with hundreds of C-level hiring managers. The process is straightforward and can be duplicated by anyone who is open to new ideas, willing to critically examine their own performance, and committed to putting in the considerable time and effort required to do things right. Although my thoughts on the topic have been developed through my work recruiting senior executives, the principles can be applied to hiring professionals at any level.

The six steps look simple, but that's an illusion. Executing them well is challenging and complex.

*Step 1: Defining the job.* Defining the job means committing to paper the details of the position and the ideal candidate profile. Less obviously, it also means making sure the key players are in agreement before you leave the starting line. While it may seem painfully clear that you can't find what you're looking for if you don't know what you want, this is one of the most common areas where hiring managers stumble.

*Step 2: Finding candidates.* No search can succeed without an adequate supply of candidates to evaluate. Nowadays technologies like LinkedIn have made it easier than ever to identify potential candidates, but that's merely a start. The best candidates have the most employment options, and the hard part is convincing them to talk with you. Bringing them to the table requires a persuasive presentation of the hiring company and the open position.

*Step 3: Interviewing.* The interview is a rich opportunity to learn about the candidate, her skills and accomplishments, and her compatibility with your organization's values and culture. However, most hiring managers don't have a systematic approach to the interview, and as a result they learn far less about candidates than they should. That can leave them with incomplete or faulty data when it comes time to make decisions.

*Step 4: Referencing.* References are a unique opportunity to get third-party testimony about the candidate's strengths and weaknesses, and valuable information on how best to manage the candidate after he comes aboard. Yet despite their obvious importance, references are perhaps the most neglected aspect of hiring. All too often they are treated as a formality rather than as an integral part of the process.

*Step 5: Making the offer.* Making an offer that's accepted involves far more than getting the numbers right. Expectations have to be set up-front, the offer has to be presented in a way that makes the candidate feel valued and wanted, and negotiations must be handled in a fashion that doesn't agitate either party. It's a delicate process, and there are almost innumerable ways for a promising candidacy to derail.

*Step 6: Onboarding.* What's that, you didn't know there's anything to be done after the hire? You're not alone. Onboarding refers to any type of program designed to rapidly integrate new executives and teach them the inside information they'll need to be successful. Most companies provide little to no assistance to new executives, and as a result many who would otherwise have been successful founder and fail.

At this moment you may be thinking, "Those steps are obvious. This book is too basic." I concede that the steps are simple and may seem obvious to many people. However, it's self-evident that most executives have not come close to mastering these steps. Like most things in business, the concepts are simple, but the execution is hard. If you are a golfer, you know that developing a great swing is simple in theory, but impossible to master without dedication and the help of a good coach. So it is with hiring.

Let's take just one example, definition of the job. Defining the job would seem to be a simple enough task, but many hiring managers get it wrong. Starting with a poorly defined job or a weak definition of the ideal candidate is like building a house on a bad foundation. Odds are the house will never get completed, and if it does, there's a likelihood it will have to be torn down.

There are two common scenarios. In the first, the hiring manager is so eager to get going that he starts recruiting before he really knows what he wants. Of course there is a written job description, but it is imprecise, ambiguous, or simply missing key points. During the search, the hiring manager continually vacillates on key aspects of the specification. Since he doesn't know what he's looking for, these searches usually drag on and on. I call them "Goldilocks searches" because this candidate is too hot, that one is too cold, and none is ever just right.

In the second scenario, the hiring manager knows exactly what she's looking for, but fails to build consensus with key players in the organization. The search sails along until candidates start interviewing and it becomes apparent that everyone is looking for something different. In the worst case, the hiring manager takes the search to what appears to be its conclusion, only to have her choice vetoed by a boss or board member who has other ideas.

Here's another example, this time related to interviewing. We have all known hiring managers who ask strange interview questions that they believe open a window into a candidate's deeper personality and way of thinking. Usually these are profoundly silly. I like to call them "magic questions" because those who use them believe they gain an almost magical insight on candidates. Sadly, they are only half right. The questions do provide deep insight, but not into the candidate. Rather, they serve notice that the interviewer still has a lot to learn.

There's no shortage of examples, from my personal favorite, "If you were an animal, which one would you be?" to "Whom do you most admire from history?" Absurd questions like these teach nothing about the candidate and make the interviewer look foolish. The best candidates will run for the exits, leaving the interviewer with those who are lacking in self-respect or just really need a job.

By now it should be clear that the six steps aren't as simple as they first appeared. I could go on with more examples, but that's why I wrote the rest of this book. *Mastering the Art of Recruiting* provides easy-to-follow instructions on how to get things right the first time, every step of the way. It also maps out the most common ways hiring managers make mistakes, so you can avoid them.

## Five Commonsense Principles for Recruiting Success

Some years ago I read an interesting interview with a well-known bluegrass fiddle player, a former child prodigy now in her forties, who talked about how her playing has changed over the course of her career. As a youngster, she focused on playing lots of notes and playing fast, but as she got older she began to focus more and more on simplicity. She said (and I roughly paraphrase), "It used to be about adding as much as possible, but now it's taking things out and getting to the essentials."

It struck me that this is a great example of how we become expert at anything. In the beginning, when learning something new, everything looks complicated. Sometimes the complexity keeps increasing as we learn more facts and skills. But eventually, in an interesting reversal, everything starts to get easier. As we gain expertise, what was once complex becomes simple. We can see the big picture and reduce a topic to its essence.

I've experienced this in my own work as an executive search consultant. At first, the process seemed endlessly complex, and the human dynamics of hiring often felt like a psychological Rubik's cube. Now, after almost two decades recruiting board members, general management, and functional leaders, I can see the core principles with clarity. It all seems much simpler.

Over those years, I've identified five principles that guide my recruiting work. I share them here for two reasons. First, they contain a hopeful message that should be encouraging to anyone who is going through the hard work of improving their hiring results, or is thinking about starting on that path. Second, keeping these principles in mind as you are recruiting will help you stay on track when it feels like you're losing your way.

*Principle 1: The basics of good hiring are common sense—accessible to anyone who is willing to work hard.* This is great news for anyone who wants to improve. You don't need to be born with any special abilities to excel at hiring. All that's required is dedication and the willingness to put in the time and effort.

*Principle 2: Success is the result of executing many small tasks.* When you look closely at the hiring process, you see that it consists of a chain of countless small items. The quality of the entire process is only as strong as the weakest link, so details matter. You must focus on following the process, avoid skipping steps, and dedicate yourself to doing a great job on each one of them.

*Principle 3: Hiring requires good judgment about people, and it's a skill anyone can master.* This flies in the face of conventional wisdom, because we're accustomed to thinking of people skills as a fixed personality trait. That kind of thinking makes many hiring managers despair of their prospects of mastering the hiring process. But the fact is that anyone can develop outstanding skill over time, through the disciplined and consistent application of a sound hiring process. That's an incredibly hopeful message.

*Principle 4: Successful hiring requires a significant time investment.* Every executive I know is juggling dozens of competing priorities, and there is never enough time in the day. It's tempting to look for shortcuts, but there are none. You must be willing to put in the time to do it right. After all, we've already established that finding great people is your number-one business problem.

The good news is that the time you invest in hiring the right people yields an outsized return. Great people make everything run better, and you'll save incalculable hours by avoiding management crises.

## FIVE COMMONSENSE PRINCIPLES FOR RECRUITING SUCCESS

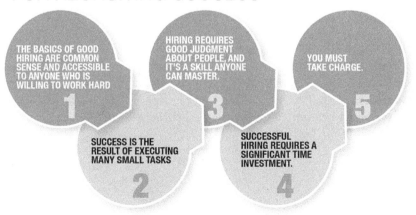

*Principle 5: You must take charge.* To paraphrase a famously ungrammatical statement from a former president, "You are the decider." If you have support from a strong human resources professional or recruiter (or both), consider yourself fortunate, but don't expect these people to do your job. They can provide expert counsel and execute many tasks on your behalf, but there are other times where your personal involvement is essential. There's a limit to how much you can delegate. At all stages of the hiring process you must keep your hands firmly on the reins, provide clear direction, and make timely decisions. Otherwise the process will fail to move forward.

## Thoughts on Using This Book

The structure of the book is straightforward. A full chapter is devoted to each of the six steps of the hiring process, in chronological order, from defining the job to onboarding executives. This allows for detailed instruction on how to get things right. Additional chapters focus on developing the mindset you'll need for recruiting, diagnosing and fixing common problems, and developing mastery over time.

One final thought: I know you are busy, and I promise to respect your time. Many of my clients won't read a long business book. Indeed, my own shelves are full of books that were too boring or academic to be worth any more than a quick skim. That's why this book is designed as a practical manual that can be read in one or two sittings. It is short and easy to read, with a focus on providing immediately actionable advice. Each chapter ends with a summary of key points that are intended to make it easy to refer back to the book over time.

## Notes

1. Joseph Daniel McCool, *Deciding Who Leads: How Executive Recruiters Drive, Direct & Disrupt the Global Search for Management Talent* (Mountain View: Davies-Black, 2008), 109.

2. Malcolm Gladwell, *Blink: The Power of Thinking Without Thinking* (Back Bay Books/Little, Brown and Company, 2007), 13. Gladwell introduces the term "rapid cognition" on page 13 and explores it throughout the rest of the book.

# Chapter 2

# Attitude Adjustment: Get in the Recruiting Mindset

My friend Dan was telling the story of a recent interview. He seemed equally annoyed and amused by the unusual meeting.

"That was the strangest interview I have ever been on. That guy is a piece of work!"

"That guy" was the CEO of a white-hot computing company that was growing revenue at a triple-digit annual rate. It was one of those rare start-ups where everything was going right. The company was searching for a sales and marketing leader to help scale the business and maintain or even accelerate its impressive growth trajectory. The idea was that the new VP, along with the addition of other seasoned executives, would complement the CEO, who was immensely talented but relatively inexperienced.

Dan was a seasoned executive with an outstanding track record. He was known and respected by several members of the hiring company's board. He was exactly the sort of person the company needed to attract if it hoped to continue its winning streak. What did the CEO say to provoke such a negative reaction?

Dan explained, "The guy was almost hostile. As soon as we sat down, he told me he's not looking for anyone with ideas. He told me he's a marketing guy and he's never met a marketing person who's as good as he is. Then he said he's already figured out the marketing plan, and he just wants someone to execute it. If that's the deal, I don't know why he's looking at people like me. He really wants to run sales and marketing himself. If that's true, all he needs is a low-level person to do what he tells them to do."

Dan withdrew gracefully, but he followed the company's progress. The search continued, and a few more talented candidates fell by the wayside in similar fashion, as the CEO made it clear their ideas weren't wanted. They ended up with someone far less capable than my friend, but with a more pliable spine.

Since you are reading this book, you want to recruit great people for your organization. The competition for the best talent is stiff, no matter the state of the overall economy. What can you do to maximize your odds of winning in the battle for talent? How can you avoid turning off good candidates, as the CEO did in our story?

You can start by assessing the way you approach hiring executive-level talent. A precondition for hiring great people is what I call the *recruiting mindset*. It's a set of attitudes and behaviors that help attract the very best people and make searches run well. They are described in detail in this chapter. But before we get to them, let's take a moment to consider what great candidates want.

## What Attracts Top Talent?

I am an enthusiastic (though not very skilled) fly fisherman. Anglers know fish are very selective when feeding, and the biggest fish are the pickiest of all. They've grown bigger by virtue of their superior judgment—they're not easily fooled, and they won't bite just anything. At any moment they will be feeding on a short list of items, usually a particular species of insect in a specific phase of its life cycle. If you don't have what they want, presented to them in exactly the right way, you will work for hours with no result. You'll have a nice day on the river or lake, but you won't catch anything.

So it is with recruiting. If you want to catch talented employees, you must understand what they want, what motivates them, and why they might want to come to work for you. The best talent is also the most selective. If you don't have what it takes to attract them, you won't catch them, and unlike fishing, you won't even have a nice day spent in the outdoors to show for it.

Consider the goals of elite performers, the ones you would like to join your team. What do they look for when changing jobs? While every candidate has a unique set of motivations and goals, there are a few common threads that tie together top performers, and they can be summarized in four simple points.

First, the very best people are *exceptionally thoughtful* in making job changes. They view their careers almost as long-term military campaigns, and plot them out with the same great thought and precision as a general. They want every new position to be a step forward in the plan they have created for their own advancement. Every new job must contribute to career growth in a meaningful way.

Second, they want to join a company with a *promising future*. That can mean different things to different people, depending on an individual's objectives. For some it means a Fortune 100 company, for others a startup, and for yet others it might mean a turnaround. Whatever the case, the best people must see opportunity for advancement and financial reward. They won't join a laggard that's unlikely to improve. Those companies are for lesser performers who don't have as many options.

Third, the best people want *interesting and challenging work*. They want to be stretched and gain new skills. They are not interested in making lateral moves that amount to doing the same old job in a new place. That's boring, doesn't add to their repertoire of skills, and doesn't provide career advancement.

Finally, great people want to work for *effective leaders*. For our purposes—executive hiring—the basics are fairly simple. The best people want to work for strong leaders who provide clear direction and who give the executive team freedom to do their jobs without micromanagement. They want to work for leaders who foster a culture of teamwork. And they want to work for leaders from whom they can learn something—who will help them advance their own careers.

The corollary is that great people will not work for weaklings. Some weaklings don't have enough intellectual horsepower. Others don't or can't provide clear direction, or constantly change their minds—like a squirrel that cannot decide whether it wants to cross the road. Some weak leaders—like screamers, control freaks, or those who lack empathy or basic ethics—seem to be psychologically damaged.

Now that we have considered the candidate's objectives, think about what's happening in a first interview. Just as you are evaluating the candidate during that first meeting, she is evaluating you and your company.

## WHAT DO TOP PERFORMERS WANT?

| CAREER ADVANCEMENT | WORK AT A PROMISING COMPANY | INTERESTING AND CHALLENGING WORK | A GREAT BOSS AND TALENTED COLLEAGUES |

Before she walks in the door, she has done extensive research on your company and you. If the company is public, she has pored over your SEC filings. If you are privately held, she has been through your website and everything else she can find. She has also reached out to people in her network who know you, to get a feel for your reputation.

During the interview, she will be asking herself whether you are the type of person for whom she would like to work. She will be looking for clues about your management style, attitudes, and personality.

Look at your own company and yourself from a candidate's point of view. Are you offering the kind of opportunity that will attract top talent? Are you the kind of manager for whom the best people want to work?

## The Recruiting Mindset

In my years as an executive search consultant, I've been fortunate to work with some outstanding hiring managers. The best of them are distinguished by their ability to attract, assess, and select great people with skill, decisiveness, and efficiency. Their hiring "batting averages" are well above the norm. I've learned from all of them.

These standouts are a diverse group of unique individuals with vastly different personalities and management styles. They work in a wide variety

### FIVE CHARACTERISTICS OF EXECUTIVES WITH THE RECRUITING MINDSET

1. THEY UNDERSTAND THE BALANCE OF BUYING AND SELLING.

2. THEY MAKE THE SEARCH A PRIORITY.

3. THEY TREAT PEOPLE WELL.

4. THEY GET HELP FROM A RECRUITING PARTNER.

5. THEY ASK FOR HELP.

of businesses and functions. Yet in spite of their differences, when it comes to hiring they have a lot in common.

Great hiring managers share a set of beliefs and behaviors I call the *recruiting mindset*. People who have the recruiting mindset hire great people, and those who don't, fail—even when they are in strong businesses that should be able to attract top talent. The recruiting mindset consists of five traits, each of which is described below. Having some but not all of these traits isn't good enough—all are required to conduct a successful search that ends in the hiring of a great individual.

As you read the list, ask yourself whether you share these traits. If you do, you are already on the right track. If you don't, it's time to adjust your approach to recruiting before you launch the next search for a member of your team. Make note of the areas where you need to improve, and revisit the list over time to monitor your own progress.

1. *Great hiring managers understand the balance of buying and selling.*

Hiring, like many other business transactions, is a delicate balance of buying and selling. You are evaluating candidates, but they are also evaluating you. If you aren't sensitive to this fact and approach the process only as a buyer, without regard to the goals and interests of candidates, you will fail.

The process of dating (something most of us have endured) provides some instructive parallels. During a first date, each side wants to appeal to the other, while simultaneously evaluating the other person. Both people are asking themselves, "Am I making a positive impression?" and "Do I want to meet this person again?" If things go well, there's another date, and both sides get to know each other a little bit better. If that goes well, the dance continues, and if the courtship goes on the process may end in a marriage.

It's easy to see the parallels with interviewing. Candidates work hard to impress hiring managers with their skills and accomplishments, but they are simultaneously evaluating the company, job, and hiring manager. For his part, the hiring manager is forming an opinion of the candidate's background and fit with the organization, and at the same time selling the candidate on the opportunity. When things go well, there is a respectful balance of buying and selling on both sides.

Now imagine a first interview where neither party respected this delicate give and take. The hiring manager might say, "You probably already know how lucky and privileged you are that I've agreed to this interview. Now, prove to me why I should hire you!" Or the candidate might begin with, "I have an incredible track record, and frankly you would be lucky if I decide to work here. So why would I? What's so great about this company and this job? And by the way, are you the kind of star for whom I want to work?" Those interviews would be disastrous, and there would be no second meeting.

As the hiring manager, you have two goals for the introductory interview. First, you need to learn enough about the candidate—both his experience and his personality—to determine whether it is worthwhile to continue discussions. Second, you must make the most compelling case possible for the company and the position you are trying to fill. You want to enhance the candidate's interest so he leaves the meeting wanting to learn more. If everything goes well, you will agree to have another set of meetings and perhaps include a few key members of your team.

Many readers will find this obvious, but I've seen countless hiring managers get it wrong. The most common mistake is spending the entire meeting delving into the candidate's background, without spending any time selling the company and the job or providing a candidate with an opportunity to ask questions. Hiring managers who make this mistake risk coming off as arrogant and disrespectful. They also miss out on the opportunity to learn from the candidate's questions, which always provide a window into his thinking and motivations.

Less commonly, the interview is imbalanced in the other direction, and the hiring manager spends so much time talking about the company and the position that she fails to learn much about the person she is interviewing. A candidate once told me, "The interview went okay, but I felt uneasy about it. He spent the entire time talking, and he didn't learn very much about me." Ironically, many of the hiring managers who make this mistake later complain that the candidate did not have much to say. No doubt they would have said more if the conversation had been more of a dialogue.

Here's a rather extreme example to illustrate what can go wrong. A friend was consulting with the CEO of a promising startup, who was recruiting for a key executive position. The company had developed what appeared to be a very promising potential therapy for a widespread chronic condition, and the CEO was able to convince a small parade of highly qualified people to interview.

Not one of them agreed to a second interview. Why? The CEO conducted the initial interview like an inquisition. He grilled them in a way that suggested profound disrespect, as if his starting assumption was that each candidate had no redeeming qualities unless they could prove otherwise.

The candidates, as good ones always do, had done their homework and came prepared with detailed and perceptive questions. Rather than viewing their preparation and insight as positives (which they certainly were), the CEO saw many of the questions as insults that implicitly questioned him or his business plan.

On the surface, hiring people looks like a buying transaction. But it's never that simple, especially when it comes to top executive talent. The entire process is a delicate dance of buying and selling, and both parties must be convinced that working together makes sense. Of course, the scales will tip one way or another as the hiring manager and candidate get to know one another better and the process advances, but it is never one-sided. Getting the balance of buying and selling right and remaining sensitive to the candidate's objectives is essential. Without it, you will never get to a deal.

2. *The best hiring managers make the search a priority.*

As an executive search consultant, I wake up every morning with one simple objective: to recruit great candidates.

For the busy executives who are my clients, however, it's a lot more complicated. They are juggling dozens of competing priorities, plus the unplanned emergencies that inevitably arise from time to time in any business. Recruiting is one of their top priorities, of course, but it is one of many. They do not have the luxury of focusing on recruiting in the same way that I do. Yet the best of them, those who truly excel at recruiting executive-level talent, understand that building a great team is the single most important thing they can do to make themselves successful, and they make sure they give it the attention it requires and deserves.

It's easy to let the tasks of recruiting slide. Faced with a daily barrage of important issues demanding attention, it's tempting to push recruiting activities to the bottom of the to-do list. Recruiting is a long-term project, and like other long-term initiatives it can take a backseat to short-term issues that appear, at least in the moment, to be more important. The hiring manager rationalizes, "What's one more day when it comes to scheduling an interview, providing feedback on a resume to the recruiting partner, or making a yes/no decision on a candidate?" Then tomorrow arrives with a new set of "hot" issues, and the cycle repeats itself. The same thing happens the next day, and the day after that, and before you know it, the tiny delays have snowballed and significantly slowed down the recruiting process.

"That won't happen," you may say to yourself. "I delegated the search to an executive recruiter, or to an internal HR executive. They'll just get it done."

Not so fast. Those recruiting partners will provide essential help, but they can't do it alone, and great hiring managers intuitively understand why. The objective of the search is to hire a member of your staff, and only you can make the decisions that move things forward and ultimately result in a hire. You must define the criteria you'll use for evaluation, provide feedback on candidates, make any needed midcourse corrections as you refine your requirements, and make yes-or-no decisions on candidates. You don't want an executive recruiter for someone on your HR team making those decisions for you.

Yes, you can and should put an executive recruiter or HR executive in charge of the search for a new member of your team. They will do hundreds of hours of legwork, provide you with good advice, and push you for feedback when it's needed to keep things moving. But in the end, they are service providers who are there to make your vision a reality. You are still leading the recruiting project, and your active involvement and prompt attention, when needed, are essential and will make the difference between success and failure.

What happens if you are not appropriately engaged in the search process? The failure of an executive to be sufficiently involved in recruiting can have two highly undesirable consequences that can kill a search.

First, when the hiring manager is disengaged, the recruiter or HR partner doesn't have enough information to do his or her job effectively. The recruiting partner is a proxy for the hiring manager and, as such, cannot do an effective job without clear direction and continual feedback. When the hiring manager is disengaged, this doesn't happen. There is a flurry of recruiting activity, but it's misdirected and ultimately unproductive. Imagine a rocket that blasts off with a dysfunctional guidance system. There's a dramatic launch, tons of fuel are burned, and the team celebrates what they think is an auspicious beginning. But then the rocket begins a slow, inexorable drift off-course that ends in a devastating crash.

Second, a disengaged hiring manager is the source of endless delays. He does not provide timely feedback on candidates or schedule interviews promptly. Small delays quickly add up to weeks or even months. Indeed, the failure of a hiring manager to attend to decisions promptly is the most common source of delays in recruiting.

There's another, more insidious fallout from these delays. Great candidates have a shelf life. They have other opportunities, and they are not sitting on their hands waiting for you to act. If you don't make decisions, the candidate will make them for you. Further, delays can send a message to candidates that you aren't very excited about them. Whether you intend it or not, delays telegraph ambivalence, and good candidates get the message they should move on.

The best hiring managers, those with the recruiting mindset, put hiring at the top of the to-do list. They don't delay interviewing candidates, giving feedback, or making decisions. They know that a string of small delays will quickly combine to slow the entire process by weeks or months. They know that, even when assisted by a recruiting professional, they must captain the recruiting effort and stay firmly in charge.

3. *Excellent hiring managers treat people well.*

Mothers counsel, "Treat other people the way you would like to be treated." Executives with the recruiting mindset follow this advice in their interactions with candidates. That means treating them with respect during interviews, responding to them in a timely way, and letting them know where they stand in the process. These courtesies were once commonplace, but in recent years they have declined. This is partly due to the accelerating pace of business life, and partly because power in hiring interactions swung so strongly toward employers in the wake of the 2008 economic crisis. Whatever the reasons, the trend is quite real.

Leaving questions of etiquette aside, employers who treat candidates well earn a rich return. Candidates who have been treated well during the interview process and salary negotiations are far more likely to accept an offer. They begin a new job with energy and enthusiasm, free of misgivings and doubts. The other candidates, the ones who lost out on the position, will feel they were treated fairly and with respect. Although understandably disappointed, they exit the interviewing process with a positive impression of the company and the individuals they have met.

Over time the benefits of treating people well accumulate as you and your company earn a reputation for treating potential employees with respect. That reputational equity, though difficult to quantify in dollars, is nonetheless incredibly valuable. It can turn your company and you into magnets that attract talent.

Now let's consider what happens when candidates feel they are treated poorly. Candidates who are not treated well are far more likely to drop out of the interviewing process. Further, they are far less likely to accept an offer if one is extended. Quite rightly, they assume that things will probably only get worse if they are hired. The very best candidates are the first to go. When they do, they tell their friends that interviewing at your company was a horror show.

Who is left? Candidates who tolerate poor treatment from a prospective employer usually don't have a choice. They are people who need a job (and thus are reluctant to walk away from any opportunity), those with damaged self-esteem, or lesser talents without other options.

Those are the short-term costs, but the long-term toll is arguably far higher. In the long run, companies and hiring managers that fail to treat candidates well earn a reputation that repels good people. Think for a moment and I'm sure that you can quickly name companies and individuals for whom you would never consider working. They've earned a reputation so bad that you won't even talk with them. They have crippled their ability to hire great people, and when that happens it's almost impossible to recover.

By now it should be clear that treating people well is in your business interest. But what exactly does it mean to treat people well in the context of their candidacy for a position at your company? In my opinion there are four simple guidelines.

First, you must be prepared for the interview. That sounds basic, and it is, but I have spoken with countless executives who have been interviewed by people who invested no time in preparing for the meeting. They have not read the candidate's resume, know little to nothing about his or her background, and sometimes (in cases where the interviewer is not the hiring manager) they don't even know much about the job for which the candidate is interviewing. These interviews are a waste of time for all sides.

Second, it's important to go into the interview with the assumption that the candidate is a competent individual. Indeed, if they have made it through the screening process and earned a face-to-face interview, they

## WHAT DOES IT MEAN
## TO TREAT CANDIDATES WELL?

| BE PREPARED FOR THE INTERVIEW | ASSUME THE CANDIDATE IS COMPETENT UNTIL SHOWN OTHERWISE | RESPECT THE BALANCE OF BUYING AND SELLING | KEEP THEM INFORMED OF WHERE THEY STAND |
| --- | --- | --- | --- |

should be. Yet some hiring managers enter an interview as if it were an interrogation for the Inquisition. They take an arrogant and vaguely hostile approach to questioning that subtly says to the candidate, "Prove to me you are not an idiot." Candidates usually conclude that the interviewer is the idiot and don't come back.

Third, as detailed above, you must respect the balance of buying and selling. Take time to understand the candidate's career objectives and how the position you are trying to fill might satisfy her. Give her ample time to ask questions (which, by the way, provide insight into her level of preparation and general business acumen). Showing the candidate that you recognize she is also a buyer demonstrates respect.

Finally, keep candidates informed throughout the process. If a candidate fails to advance to the next round of interviews and you have decided to eliminate him from consideration, let him know with a phone call. Candidates who remain under consideration should be kept regularly informed of where they stand and your expected timetable for completing the search. If you are working with an executive search consultant or an HR professional, they should do this for you.

Treating people well does not mean you can make everyone happy. A search is a contest with one winner, and the other candidates will be disappointed with the outcome. You can't change that, but you can aspire to make everyone who engages with you feel that they have been treated fairly.

One final thought: treating people well does not mean you cannot conduct a tough interview. In fact, candidates—especially the best ones—will expect it. An intelligent, probing, and challenging interview will earn you their respect, and be seen by candidates as a very positive sign. The corollary is also true: the best candidates will view a weak or unchallenging interview as a red flag. They will wonder whether you are an effective leader.

4. *Great hiring managers get help from a recruiting partner.*

A thorough and well-run search for an executive takes hundreds of hours, and busy hiring managers don't have the time required to do it all on their own. Executives with the recruiting mindset know this, and they delegate management of the search to a trusted partner. Whether it's an HR executive or an executive search professional, a good recruiting partner frees the hiring manager from the laborious and sometimes tedious work of creating a slate of candidates, so she can focus on the one area where her involvement is essential—making decisions.

Many executives at companies with tight budgets try to go it alone. Understandably, they want to keep expenses under control. Usually they canvas their network for referrals, and occasionally those efforts get results. But just as often they don't, and the hiring manager is faced with a decision. Should he commit the considerable cash resources to conduct an executive search, should he try to go it alone, or should he use an internal resource?

Consider what's involved in a typical executive search. Today, thanks to resources like LinkedIn, identification of potential candidates can be done quickly by almost anyone. It's not hard; almost anyone could build a reasonable target list in a couple of hours.

But that doesn't get you anywhere. The next step—which is very hard indeed—is talking with prospective candidates and convincing them to come to the table. That process requires hundreds of phone calls and hundreds of hours. Then come many more hours of phone and in-person interviews designed to narrow the field to the best five or six candidates.

It's probably safe to assume you do not have several hundred free hours on your calendar, so finding a partner who can help with the search is essential. Some larger companies have excellent internal recruiting groups, and if you are lucky enough to have that resource, it may solve your problem. Most companies, however, have HR groups that are stretched incredibly thin. They can't help with a project on the scale of an executive search.

The other option is to hire an executive search consultant. Executive search firms are structured to provide precisely the type of intensive, project-based effort that is required. As an executive recruiter, I must confess to having a strong bias. In the vast majority of situations, I believe search consultants are the best way to solve the problem of recruiting executive talent.

The most common argument made against using executive search is the expense, but this is short-term and narrow thinking. Yes, executive search is expensive, but the value returned to the company by recruiting the best possible executive is tens or even hundreds of times the cost of the service. You probably would not forgo the use of outside lawyers for litigation or intellectual property matters. The professionals who recruit talent are just as essential, and arguably return even greater value.

The lesson is that you cannot recruit executive-level talent on your own. You must get help from an HR professional or an executive recruiter. Without them, you won't be able to mount a serious campaign, and your efforts will have a low probability of success.

5. *The best hiring managers ask for advice.*

Effective leaders are keenly aware they don't have all the answers. They build a "brain trust" of mentors and trusted colleagues with whom they can consult when they are confronting challenging issues. They have maturity and self-confidence, and that makes them open to asking for help, listening to advice, and integrating the ideas of others when they make sense. Executives with the recruiting mindset are constantly asking themselves, "How can I improve?"

Indeed, there are few aspects of business where asking for help is more important than in recruiting. As pointed out earlier, very few young executives receive meaningful training in how to hire people. That means you must take charge of your own education. There are many options, but getting help from trusted colleagues and advisors is one of the most effective ways to accelerate learning and avoid costly and unnecessary mistakes.

Consider the constant learning required of a fast-track executive. Each step forward presents a steep and daunting learning curve. Every new job and new company presents novel challenges, and the most dangerous of them are unknown. To quote the old commonplace expression, "You don't know what you don't know." Inability to learn quickly is one of the most common reasons executives fail. But how can anyone learn fast enough to stay on the fast track?

Mentors are the answer to that question. A seasoned, successful executive who has been in your shoes is an indispensable guide. An effective mentor will help you navigate difficult business problems and anticipate looming challenges you don't know exist. He will help you focus on your strengths and shore up your weaknesses. He will give you the hard advice you may not want to hear, and he will do it in an honest, safe, and confidential forum, far from the scrutiny of superiors and peers.

What types of mentors are most helpful when it comes to recruiting? Any seasoned executive can help, but I strongly believe that everyone should have an HR executive in their stable of advisors. Not just any HR executive, but one of those rarities who has been a valued partner to the executives he has served.

The archetypical example is a friend of mine, whom I'll call Jim. After a corporate career that culminated in his work as vice president of human resources at a prominent pharmaceutical company, Jim launched a consulting practice in which he focuses on providing HR strategy to startup CEOs. He has helped dozens of leaders build their teams and has seen every scenario one could imagine—plus many one could not! He has many times more hiring experience than any of the CEOs he serves. He gives them advice that keeps them on track, helps them recruit the best possible people, and gives them a much higher probability of business success.

The lesson is simple. If you are not getting help, change that starting today. Cultivate mentors who can help you accelerate learning and stay on the fast track, and then actively seek out their advice. Even elite athletes who are the best in the world at what they do know they will perform better with the help of a coach. Phil Mickelson takes advice on his golf swing, and Serena Williams is coached on her serve. Are you so good that you couldn't benefit from the advice of a mentor?

Now that we have covered the basics, it's time to dive into the search process. We'll begin the process in the next chapter with a discussion of creating the position description and candidate specification.

## Summary

Executives who excel at hiring top talent share five attitudes and behaviors:

- *They understand the balance of buying and selling.* Interviewing is a two-way street. Just as the hiring manager is evaluating the candidate, the candidate is evaluating her. The hiring manager must sell the company, the job, and herself.
- *They make the search of priority.* Busy executives have dozens of competing priorities, but those who make great hiring decisions put recruiting at the top of the to-do list.
- *They treat people well.* An effective hiring manager treats candidates with respect and keeps them informed about their progress. He wants all of the candidates to exit the process with a positive impression of himself and the company.
- *They get help from a recruiting partner.* The best hiring managers know it's impossible to conduct a thorough executive search on their own. They get help from a senior-level HR executive or an executive search consultant.
- *They ask for advice.* Effective hiring managers know they don't have all the answers. They develop a network of trusted colleagues and mentors, and actively solicit their advice.

## Chapter 3

# Seek and You Shall Find (If You Know What You're Looking For)

As a young man I had a terrible time buying gifts for other people. And it was never worse than at Christmas.

I would return from college with only a few days for shopping. I'd set out for the local stores in the firm belief I knew what to get for my parents and siblings—I had a list! But in truth my ideas were vague and unfocused. I'd get to a store and wander around aimlessly, hoping something would strike me as just right. That almost never happened. I kept looking.

The rapid approach of Christmas provided a hard deadline for my efforts. I could not show up empty-handed; that would not have made me popular with my family. I had to get the shopping done, but I held out hope I'd find the perfect gifts. As the clock ticked on, I got more and more nervous.

On Christmas Eve, the imminent closure of stores would force me to act. Sometimes I got lucky, but more often than not the gifts I bought were an unsatisfying compromise. I had hoped the presents would be meaningful, something the recipients would really want and appreciate. But I fell far short of that goal.

In hindsight, I realize that I was such an ineffective shopper because I didn't know what I wanted. I thought I had a plan, but my ideas were too vague and didn't give me concrete objectives. In the absence of clearly defined goals, my quest dragged on and on. For example, my list might say "Buy Dad clothing." That's quite open-ended, and I'd visit countless men's stores looking for nothing in particular. I needed something a lot more specific, like "Get Dad a Nike golf shirt." My shopping expedition was destined to fail from the start because I hadn't thought it through in sufficient detail. It's common sense that you can't find something if you don't know what you're looking for.

If you think of hiring a new executive as shopping, it's easy to see the parallels with the lessons I learned as a college student at Christmas. If you begin the search for a new executive with poorly defined goals, you will find yourself wandering aimlessly from candidate to candidate, just as I wandered from store to store. You will meet far more candidates than necessary, and wonder why none of them meets expectations. The search will drag on, and pressure will mount as the company continues to operate without the needed executive's leadership, and your superiors begin to wonder whether you know what you're doing. Eventually, the pressure to fill the job may lead you to offer the position to a candidate who is an unsatisfying compromise.

One sure sign a hiring manager is headed for trouble is when he says he wants to recruit a "rock star." In recruiting, no single term is more common or more dangerous. (There are endless variations on this theme. A football fan told me he wanted a Tom Brady; a hockey fanatic said he needed Mario Lemieux. You get the picture.)

"Rock star" is an empty platitude, the equivalent of "Buy Dad an awesome gift" on my Christmas shopping list. "I want a rock star" means "I want to hire an exceptional performer." That's nice, but doesn't everyone? Does anyone set out to hire a new executive who's mediocre or downright incompetent? I can assure you that no one has ever retained my firm and asked us to target the bottom of the talent pool.

"Rock star" and similar terms are dangerous because they often mask a failure to think through what's really needed in candidates. It's easy for the executive team, or the Board of Directors, or anyone else to agree that the company needs a rock star. It's much more difficult to agree on what that means.

## The Specification

In recruiting, the parallel to my Christmas shopping list is the specification. The specification defines the job and the profile of ideal candidates. When a specification is done well, it establishes a clear vision that guides the entire search effort. Conversely, a poor specification provides insufficient direction that leads to ineffectual action. It's the difference between "Here's General Eisenhower's plan for the assault on Normandy" and "Hey, let's invade

Europe!" The clear goals in a good specification lead to focused planning, efficient action, and the rapid attainment of desired results.

Keep it short—ideally the specification should be no more than a single page. It's easy to write a long specification that's a laundry list of job tasks and candidate requirements, but you need to emphasize what's really important. Brevity will force you to boil this down. In fact, if you can't condense the specification down to a single page, it's a good sign you don't know what you want, or that you need to think more about the hierarchy of priorities.

Use simple, clear language. A specification that's full of business jargon will make it impossible to communicate your objectives to others in the company or to the candidates you hope to attract. In the worst case, readers—both inside and outside the company—will assume you are a bureaucrat if you write like one. Using simple language will force you to communicate your vision in a straightforward and cogent way.

Beware of distractions that masquerade as the specification. There's a good chance human resources will ask you for a long, detailed document that catalogs the smallest of job responsibilities and candidate requirements. In other words, they want the laundry list. Don't confuse this with the short and focused specification needed to guide your search. If HR wants a long and highly detailed list, view the document you provide them as a bureaucratic requirement, like a tax filing. Give them what they need, then forget about it and get back on track.

Drafting the specification sounds simple—after all, it's only one page! But creating this short document is deceptively complex. An effective specification is much more than words on a page; it's the end product of thoughtful deliberation and consensus building.

Forging agreement among key players within the company, not the act of writing, is always the most time consuming (and sometimes difficult) part of the process. As with most endeavors, it's the human part of the process that takes the most time and presents the most challenges. After writing the first draft of the specification, expect to take it through several revisions as you receive input from others who have a stake in the new hire, and work through disagreements. If you don't achieve consensus upfront, you will pay the price later when good candidates are rejected because interviewers are evaluating them with different criteria.

Failure to get the specification right is the most common reason searches run into trouble. However, if you invest the time to do it well, you'll set the stage for a smooth, fast, and successful search.

## Writing the First Draft

Writing the first draft of the specification will not take much time, provided you have given thought to the issues and have a clear conception of priorities. Before sitting down to put words to paper, think through the following questions about the job and what you seek in candidates.

Let's start with the job description. The job description sets out the most important things about the position. These include, of course, the basic facts and figures relating to the job, such as scope of responsibilities, organizational structure, and target compensation. In addition, it should provide an overview of the job's mission by calling out short- and long-term goals, and referencing any special challenges the position will face. An effective job description answers these questions:

- *What's the organizational structure?* If this is an existing position, the structure may already be defined, but if it's new it will require thought. To what position will the job report? What is the structure of the organization the position will manage? Is there any flexibility? For example, if you are searching for a vice president of sales but find a strong candidate who has been vice president of sales and marketing, would you be open to giving the new executive both functions?
- *What are the top short-term priorities the position must accomplish?* If the function is in good shape, the goal for the first 90 to 180 days may be as simple as learning the business and organization and keeping it on track. If there are burning problems that must be immediately resolved, they should be called out. Keep it focused—there should be two or three top short-term goals, not ten.
- *What are the top long-term goals?* If successful, what will the executive have achieved at one year? Two years? Three years? Again, keep it focused.
- *Does the organization the executive will manage require major changes?* Is this an organization that must be turned around, or is this a case of continuing management of an organization that is already on the right track? Will the new executive have to build an organization from scratch, or dramatically scale it?
- *Where is the job based?* Is the job based at corporate headquarters? At another corporate location? Would you consider an executive who works remotely? Remote working arrangements for executives are usually a bad idea, but sales leaders can be an exception if they spend most of their time in the field.
- *How much travel is involved?* It's important to make expectations on travel explicit. That will help to avoid wasting time with candidates who will be unwilling or unable to travel enough to do the job effectively.

- *Who are the other executives with whom the position will work most closely?* If you are searching for an R&D leader, the answer might be the leaders of manufacturing and marketing. If you are searching for a marketing leader, it might be peers running sales and R&D.
- *What is the target compensation?* How is it structured? Exact details aren't required, but the ballpark number establishes the level of candidate you can attract, and defining it will force you to define the level of candidate you want and can afford.
- *What's the title?* Titles are a minor minefield because they vary so widely across different industries and companies. When it comes to choosing a title for the position, there are two things to keep in mind. First, the title should be consistent with the norms of your company. Second, the title must be one that will be seen as appropriate to the candidates you wish to target. For example, if a position is titled *director* and targeted candidates are primarily titled *vice president*, most prospective candidates won't even listen.

Now let's move on to the candidate profile. The candidate profile follows naturally from the job description. Armed with a clear vision of the job, it's possible to define the profile of candidates who will be best suited to the position and its unique challenges.

The candidate profile describes the ideal candidate, including years of experience, skills, industry expertise, record of achievement, education, and so on. It also describes in a general way the type of personality that will be successful in the context of the position and the company culture.

I find that most hiring managers have a mental picture of the ideal candidate, even if they haven't taken the time to articulate and analyze their thoughts. If you have one, jot down the key characteristics of your vision and use them to inform the specification.

A good candidate specification answers the following questions:

- *What industry (or industries) do candidates come from?* Is narrow industry experience required, or can you cast a wide net? The answer will probably depend a lot on the function—marketing, sales, and R&D can be quite industry-specific, but others, such as finance or human resources, tend to be highly transferable across industries.
- *What scale of management is required?* If you are looking for a vice president of manufacturing to run a 5000 person organization, the manufacturing leader at a small company who manages only 100 people won't make the grade. And the reverse may also be true: if you seek a manufacturing leader for a small company, executives who have managed far larger organizations may not have the hands-on orientation that's required.

- *How much experience is required?* Do you need someone who has "been there, done that," or are you also open to hiring a rising star? If you think you are open to hiring a rising star, do you really mean it?
- *Is global experience needed?* If you are looking for someone to run worldwide sales, experience only in North America probably won't do. And if you seek an R&D leader who will manage development operations in India, China, or elsewhere, you probably want someone who has experience managing a similar arrangement.
- *Are you willing to relocate someone, or do you wish to limit the search to locals?* Openness to relocation dramatically expands the pool of potential candidates, but it comes with significant costs and risks. We'll discuss them at length later in the book.
- *What kind of personal traits do you seek?* A new executive must be compatible with the hiring manager—they must have potential for a good working relationship. Furthermore, the candidate must be a good fit with the culture of the larger company. For example, an aggressive executive who is constantly pushing the boundaries probably won't do well at a company where slow and deliberate consensus building is valued. And the slow and deliberate consensus builder won't be valued at a company where fast action and aggressive risk-taking are the norm.

Here's an example of a short, clear, and concise position description.

---

## Chief Operating Officer

### Capital Equipment

*The Company*
We are a publicly held, market-leading manufacturer of capital equipment. The Company is profitable, had revenues of more than $500M last fiscal year, is growing rapidly (>10% annually), and has a strong balance sheet.

*The Position*
This is a new position that has been created to provide greater focus and management oversight to the Company's fast-growing operations, and to free the CEO to focus on developing new business opportunities.

The COO will lead and develop the Company's existing business, which is strong and has excellent future growth prospects owing to new

*(continued)*

products, continuing development of domestic and international distribution, and an emerging product category that has very high potential.

The COO reports to the CEO and has responsibility for core functions including worldwide sales, marketing, R&D, manufacturing, and compliance. The position will also help represent the Company to investors. Total headcount in the COO's organization is 1000+ people.

## Candidates

Candidates have the following attributes:

- Experience in the capital equipment markets;
- An outstanding track record, ideally including experience running a business as General Manager or President;
- Core strength in sales and marketing, with additional background managing operations functions, including manufacturing and R&D;
- Strategic skills combined with the ability to execute;
- High intelligence;
- An analytical approach to problem solving;
- Great interpersonal and presentation skills that foster successful interactions with colleagues, customers, and investors;
- Team player who can thrive in an informal, collaborative environment;
- Passionate, driven, leads by example.

## Building Consensus

Upon completing the first draft of the specification, many people believe they are done, and rush off to start looking for candidates. Not so fast! Completing the first draft of the specification is only the beginning. Now, the real work begins—building consensus.

Although you are the hiring manager, other key people will play a role in the process. They are not decision-makers, but you will find it difficult or impossible to extend an offer to a candidate they strongly oppose. Would you bring on an important new hire who is not supported by the board, your boss, or your peers? Doing so would set the stage for the new executive's failure. It would also require you to put your own reputation on the line, with potentially dire consequences for your career if things don't work out.

That's why it's so important to build consensus on the specification among the key players before you begin the search for a new executive. Not doing so is one of the most common reasons searches go wrong.

Failing to build consensus upfront is particularly dangerous because the problem is usually not obvious until weeks or even months have elapsed. The hiring manager forges ahead with the search in the mistaken belief that others share her vision. She is rudely awakened when feedback from interviewers is wildly inconsistent. Over time, she comes to realize that interviewers are looking for different things. They are not in agreement on what's being sought in candidates, and sometimes, especially when the position is a new one, they do not even agree on the scope of the job.

This situation is entirely avoidable if you take three simple steps. First, identify those who must be involved in the hiring process. This will always include your boss (or the board, if you are the CEO). In addition, it includes other executives who will work closely with the new hire. For example, the vice president of manufacturing may need to work closely with peers who run R&D and sales. Keep this list short and focused. The objective is to include those who have the greatest stake in the new hire. Too many people will slow things down.

Second, once you've identified the key players, ask them to review the specification. Make it clear that you want substantive feedback and that your goal is to identify and iron out areas of disagreement before you begin the search.

## CREATING THE SPECIFICATION

1 CONSIDER KEY QUESTIONS

2 WRITE FIRST DRAFT

3 IDENTIFY KEY PLAYERS

4 IN-PERSON REVIEWS OF SPECIFICATION

5 REVISE SPECIFICATION

6 REPEAT REVIEW/REVISION AS NECESSARY

You may be tempted to do it the easy way, and send the document for review via email. That's a mistake. Sending an email is like dropping the document in an old-fashioned inbox, where it could languish for days. Further, all of your reviewers are no doubt buried in email and eager to process it as quickly as possible. Asking for input via email is an invitation to a cursory and non-serious review of the material.

I urge you to do these reviews in person. Unless there are deep disagreements, a face-to-face meeting should require only 10 or 15 minutes. You'll have the focused attention of the reviewer and an opportunity to communicate why the reviewer's input is so important. You can also say (perhaps in more polite language), "Speak now or forever hold your peace." If it's not easy to schedule a face-to-face meeting—for example, if you and the reviewer are not based at the same location—do a teleconference. While it's not as good as an in-person meeting, you will have the reviewer's focused attention.

Finally, once you have gathered input from the reviewers, revise the specification to incorporate things you have agreed to add or change. Then, repeat step two and ask everyone to review the revised specification. Repeat as necessary, until major areas of disagreement have been eliminated. It's not uncommon for specifications to go through two or three revisions.

One final comment on the specification: The goal is to define things as clearly as possible, but you don't need perfection, and you don't need to lock everything down as if it were unchangeable. It's inevitable that your idea of what constitutes a perfect candidate will change as you meet people. You may even modify the definition of the job. That's to be expected when an intelligent person takes in and processes new information. In the famous words of Ralph Waldo Emerson, "A foolish consistency is the hobgoblin of little minds."

## 5 Common Mistakes

As we've seen, the process of creating the specification is simple. However, it's easy (and quite common) to make mistakes in the specification, and major ones get the search off on the wrong foot. Searching for an executive with a flawed specification is like building a house on a faulty foundation: unless you recognize the error early, you may get stuck demolishing the house and starting over again.

There are five common and serious specification mistakes that account for the majority of problems.

## 1. Target Compensation Is Too Low

Many searches get hung up because the hiring company has an unrealistic idea of what they must pay for the level of talent they wish to attract. In other words, they've deluded themselves into believing they can get champagne on a beer budget. In the real world, there is a robust market for executive talent, and there are not a lot of bargains. You get what you pay for.

If you're not sure what the market looks like for the position you wish to fill, do some research. You need to break out of the cocoon of your own company's norms and expectations, and find out what the position is worth in the marketplace. Start by reaching out to colleagues and peers in the industry for their perspectives. With luck, they will share their own experiences and give you their sense of the market.

You should also consult with your HR department, which may have access to helpful data. If they don't, or if you need more, do your own research to find compensation benchmarks—you'll find that compensation studies exist for almost every industry and function imaginable. If you have to make an argument for higher compensation to your superiors, study data is usually a lot more convincing then anecdotal evidence from colleagues and friends.

What if your research proves you are aiming for a level of talent you simply cannot afford? You could try to find that rare bargain, but that's a losing game, like looking for a needle in haystack. Get creative and figure out another way to structure the organization and get the work done using talent that you can afford. There are an infinite number of ways to skin the proverbial cat, and you'll have to find one that works within your budget.

## 2. Unrealistic Expectations

I once met a prospect who ran a small technology company. It had fewer than ten employees, and sales were quite modest. Worse, in a world of competitors that were experiencing hyper-growth, the business was flat. The company was located in a tiny, battered old metal building in the far corner of an industrial park. In short, this was not a business that was going to attract anyone who was on the fast track.

The owner wanted to hire a sales leader, but when he began to describe what he wanted, I immediately knew the situation was hopeless. What did he seek? He wanted a "Bobby Orr" (he was a hockey fan), a hotshot who was on a rapid upward career trajectory at competitors that were many times his company's size and much more successful. We talked about his expectations and whether they were reasonable. He didn't budge.

There was no way he was going to get what he wanted. His objective was totally unrealistic given the realities of his company. He wanted Bobby Orr, but he was running the Chiefs, the dysfunctional semipro hockey team featured in the Paul Newman classic *Slapshot*. Bobby Orr was not going to join the Chiefs. I politely passed on the assignment.

The sad part is there were many people who could have helped his company and would have loved to work for him. But he had convinced himself that none of them could possibly be good enough. His unrealistic aspirations undermined his stated objective—growing the company.

Some companies, like Apple and Google, are like magnets that attract talent. Others repel candidates because they've earned a reputation as employers to be avoided. Most are somewhere in the middle. As the hiring manager, you must be realistic about the attractiveness of your company and set achievable goals. If you do not, you could search forever with no result.

### 3. Failure to Think About Relocation

Are you willing to relocate someone? A quick and thoughtful response might be, "I'd rather not, but I will if I have to." That's a good start, but you need to think deeper than that. If you don't, you risk wasting precious time on candidates you cannot afford to hire.

Moving a new hire is expensive. At a minimum, the cost includes moving expenses, travel for house hunting, and perhaps temporary housing until the recruit is settled in a new home. On the high end, you can tack on realtor fees, mortgage points, or even the outright purchase of the candidate's home.

If your business is located in an area without a lot of local talent, you may be stuck relocating candidates. If that's the case, then it's a cost of doing business you have no choice but to incur. Decide what level of relocation support you are willing to provide, and then stick to it.

If you're lucky enough to be able to access a large enough pool of local talent, you may not need to consider candidates from outside your area. If you don't want to deal with the expense and risk of relocating someone, don't waste time looking at candidates who must be relocated.

The risks of relocation are substantial. In most cases you are relocating a family, not just an individual, and family dynamics are unpredictable.

Many years ago I recruited a vice president of marketing for a high-tech company, and the candidate planned to relocate from the San Francisco Bay area to Boston. After accepting the offer, he brought his wife to Boston to look for houses. They both loved the area, and everything was moving along as smoothly as I could have hoped. That is, until about three days before he was scheduled to begin his new job. He called the CEO to withdraw, and explained that his wife had had a change of heart. She'd decided she simply could not, would not, move, under any circumstances. We went back to the drawing board.

## 4. The Top-Secret Search

Sometimes companies want to run a confidential search in which the identity of the company is masked from potential candidates, at least in the early stages of discussions.

There are a number of reasons they might wish to do so. The most common is when the incumbent in the job is not aware she is about to be replaced, and there's a desire to avoid the disruption of having the job empty while a search is conducted. Occasionally, especially when a company is launching a confidential new initiative, it wants to avoid tipping off competitors, business partners, or Wall Street about what it's doing.

It's impossible to conduct a confidential search with internal resources, so by definition it must be conducted by an outside recruiter.

Before you decide that your search must be confidential, consider the downsides. There are rare circumstances where confidentiality is necessary, but in the majority of cases, it's not. I almost always urge my clients to conduct an open search. Here's why.

First, confidentiality limits your recruiter's ability to sell the company to prospective candidates, and that means some of the best candidates will not even engage in discussion. Most of the best candidates are happily employed, and it takes a compelling presentation of an opportunity to seize their attention and convince them to invest valuable time exploring a new job. Vague descriptions of a company and its business simply don't cut it. You will never know how many candidates you missed because they would not come to the table, but the impact will be material.

Second, confidentiality never sells well within your own organization. The incumbent—who, presumably, will be terminated or moved into a less-desirable position—at best will feel that you were not forthcoming. At worst, withholding information about the upcoming change will destroy your relationship, and burning professional bridges is never a good idea.

Even more important is the impact a confidential search may have on the rest of the organization. If other executives and the rank-and-file perceive that you have treated the outgoing executive poorly, they will assume they can expect the same treatment at some point in the future. You are sowing the seeds of unhappiness and distrust.

Consider the question again: does the search really have to be confidential? Given all of these downsides to conducting a top-secret search, is it really worth it? Think deeply about these issues. Often I find that the real reason an executive wants to conduct a confidential search is because he is uncomfortable delivering bad news and dealing with the complicated interpersonal fallout. If that's the issue, get over it.

## 5. Failure to Build Consensus

We've already discussed the perils of ignoring the need to build consensus. It's one of the most common reasons searches fail.

If there is a lack of consensus among interviewers, you'll find out when you begin to interview candidates. The most common symptom is when you've interviewed a parade of candidates and all are deemed unacceptable. Of course, there's a chance that whoever is sourcing candidates is doing a bad job, but it's far more likely there are disagreements among interviewers. You'll be sent back to the drawing board.

Don't let that happen to you—make sure you have carefully thought through the specification and built consensus among the key players.

## Summary

- The specification is the foundation of a successful search for a new executive.
- The specification defines the job and the experience and personal attributes you are seeking in candidates.
- Use clear language in the specification, and avoid business jargon.
- Keep the specification to one page. Brevity will force you to identify what's truly important, and communicate your vision most effectively.
- Identify the key players who will be involved in interviewing, and then make sure there is consensus among this group on the specification before you start talking with candidates.

**Chapter 4**

# Finding, Attracting, and Screening Candidates

My wife and I were on a drift boat floating down the Snake River in northwest Wyoming. With only one day for fishing, we wanted to make the most of our time, but the deck was stacked against us. For starters, we didn't have our equipment, not to mention a boat. We had zero knowledge of the area, and we were well aware of our limited skill. We knew we would have more fun, and learn more, from someone who could give us instruction.

That was where Will came in. Our guide knew every bend, every undercut bank, and every transition in that river. He knew it as one can only know it from fishing it every day.

Will also gave us advice on technique in a good-humored way. My wife was struggling with casting, and in a vain effort to get things right, she was flailing the line forward and backward in an almost endless series of false casts.

"When people do that," said Will, "usually they're trying to imitate Brad Pitt in *A River Runs Through It*. It's pretty, but I guarantee you he wasn't catching any fish. Do you see any fish up in the air?"

My wife chuckled and looked up. "No."

"I don't either. You're not going to catch fish unless you get your line down on the water." We all had a laugh, and my wife corrected her technique and started hooking fish.

We had a great time. Will freed us to focus on our objective—catching fish. He provided the local knowledge, fishing expertise, and equipment we lacked, and he gave us helpful instruction. Without him, our odds of success would have been infinitesimal. Short of moving to Wyoming and fishing the Snake every day for years, we could never duplicate his knowledge or skill.

What's the point of this fish story? Just as we needed help to make our fishing trip successful, you will need help to conduct a successful search. There's simply no way you have the time to conduct a search, and you don't have the deep expertise and market knowledge that comes from recruiting every day, either. Just as Will handled everything for us so we could focus on fishing, you need someone who can run the search process so you can focus on your objective—making decisions that result in a great hire.

Let's begin by looking at the scope of work involved in creating a short list of finalists.

## What's in a Search?

An aggressive search for a new executive requires hundreds of hours of work, and it's impossible for a busy hiring manager to do it alone. That would be a doomed effort, not to mention a profoundly poor use of the hiring manager's time. It's essential to have support from a strong internal talent acquisition group or an outside executive search consultant.

Not convinced? Let's look in more detail at the work that goes into a producing a short list of finalists for an executive-level job. For most hiring

TYPICAL SEARCH FUNNEL

CONTACTS
200–600

RESUMES REVIEWED
20-60

PHONE INTERVIEWS
25

IN-PERSON INTERVIEWS
~12

FINALISTS
4–6

managers, the process is opaque—they don't know what happens inside the recruiter's black box. For their part, executive recruiters like it that way; they want their profession to have an aura of mystery.

The truth is, what's inside the black box is neither glamorous nor exciting. Executive search, whether done by an internal or outside resource, involves hours of tedious work in the trenches. Thomas Edison famously said, "Genius is one percent inspiration, ninety-nine percent perspiration." There's a similar ratio in executive recruiting. Recruiters need brains, business acumen, and expertise to attract and assess candidates, but are only in a position to do so after putting in many hours of sweat.

Here's a simple graphic to illustrate the "funnel" of a typical search:

## Inside the Black Box

Let's consider a hypothetical example. Imagine you are the CEO of a company that manufactures fishing equipment. Your vice president of marketing has resigned unexpectedly, and you need to recruit her replacement. Though the resignation was not planned or welcome, it presents you with an opportunity to upgrade the position and add skills that will be important to making the company's future marketing initiatives successful.

You've created a thoughtful specification, you've reviewed it with a few key members of the board and one or two members of your staff, and you're ready to go. What happens between now and the time you begin to interview candidates?

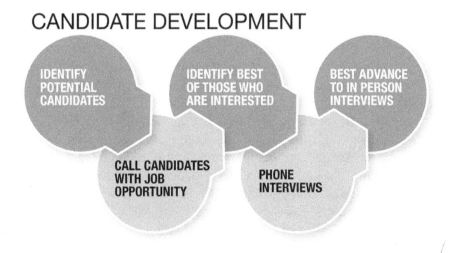

First, someone needs to identify prospective candidates. Then, someone must contact them and present a compelling picture of the opportunity and why they should take time to explore it. And finally, someone must screen interested candidates to create a short list of the very best, the ones who are worthy of the hiring manager's valuable time. All told, these tasks will require hundreds of hours of work over a 4- to 8-week period.

### Step One: Identifying Prospective Candidates

Let's begin by looking at identification of prospective candidates. Your HR staff could place an advertisement for the position, but ads would only reach people who are looking for a job. That pool is limited—and presumably you need the best talent available, whether or not they are actively looking for new employment. Reaching people who are happily employed requires hard work, first to identify them and then to contact them through a disciplined, outgoing campaign.

Identifying prospective candidates used to be difficult and time-consuming, but the rise of the Internet has made it easy. Industry associations and third parties now publish directories online, and—most important of all—LinkedIn has become the world's most comprehensive and useful database for finding potential employees. I like to say that my teenage son could build a reasonable target list for any search in a few hours.

So how is it done? Start by creating a list of target companies. In our hypothetical search, they almost certainly include other manufacturers of fishing equipment. Could it also include companies outside of fishing? What about closely related businesses, such as manufacturers of hunting equipment? Casting an even wider net might lead to including any sporting goods manufacturer, or other categories of consumer goods. Presumably the specification you've created answers these questions and provides the basis for building the list of target companies. Depending on the breadth of your definition, there could be anywhere from a dozen to hundreds.

Once the target companies are identified, the next task is to build a list of target individuals. These are people working at target companies who have job titles related to the open position—in this case, titles such as vice president or director of marketing, vice president or director of sales and marketing, and so on. Every search is different, but a marketing search like this one will commonly have anywhere from 100 to 400 individuals on the target list.

## Step Two: The Pitch

Creating a list of target individuals is the easy part. Now the real work begins—contacting them. This requires hours on phone, persuasive selling, and good judgment.

It might be tempting to use email as a time-saver, but doing so would be a serious mistake. Presenting a new job opportunity to an executive is the ultimate in high-touch selling. Recruiting at the executive level can only be done through one-to-one, personal interaction, and that means picking up the phone. Think about it—taking a position at a new company is a significant career and life decision. Asking someone to consider a new job by email or some other impersonal solicitation simply won't work.

The calls can't be delegated to junior people, either. Someone who is immediately credible on the phone must conduct them, and that means a person with seniority. Presenting a new job opportunity requires the ability to interact with the prospective candidate as a peer. You have probably received many solicitations from low-level, inexperienced recruiters, and the odds are you found them unconvincing and annoying. Is a 25-year-old with little to no business experience going to convince a senior-level executive to change the trajectory of his career?

We've established that a senior-level person must present the opportunity to prospective candidates by phone. Now it's time to consider the main points of the pitch. It's crucial to think this through carefully. An effective pitch will bring many more people to the table, while a poor one will drive down the candidate yield.

Let's return to our example of the search for a vice president of marketing at the fishing equipment manufacturer. What's attractive about the company and the job? Is the company performing well? Is it a turnaround that presents interesting challenges? Is it an industry leader, or perhaps a promising upstart? Does it have interesting or promising technology? Does the job present challenges that will be appealing to target candidates? What are the potential financial rewards for success? The recruiter must find what is most appealing about the company and job, and feature it front and center.

Now think through any objections you can foresee, and prepare responses. Has the company's performance lagged? Does it have a so-so or even negative reputation? Has there been recent bad news or even scandal? Odds are you are not faced with recruiting for a company that's been tainted like Enron or Tyco were in the early 2000s, but you may have other, less serious reputational challenges to overcome.

Once the recruiter gets on the phone, reaching prospective candidates requires great persistence. Connecting with busy executives is a challenge. Their schedules are chronically overbooked, they are often on the road, and the sheer volume of calls from recruiters has desensitized them to the presentation of new opportunities. It's not unusual to call someone three or four times before getting through.

When the recruiter does get through, the prospective candidate will evaluate the recruiter's pitch—with great skepticism—and quickly decide whether she wants to learn more. The recruiter must make a compelling case for why the candidate should explore the opportunity, communicate in a succinct and convincing way, and confidently answer questions. This requires skilled salesmanship and deep knowledge of the company and the job opportunity.

Most of the time, the initial call is brief and weighted heavily toward selling the opportunity to the potential candidate. If she is interested, she agrees to send a resume and schedule a follow-up phone call. This gives the recruiter time to study the candidate's background, and gives the candidate a chance to do research on the company. Both parties are then well prepared for a more detailed discussion.

What kind of response rate should be expected? The yield from these calls varies depending on the attractiveness of the job and demand for the function being recruited. That said, in a typical search 8 to 12 percent of contacts will be interested enough to send a resume. The yield will be lower if relocation is involved, and higher if the position is exceptionally attractive. The quality of the pitch can push the yield dramatically in either direction. Good salesmanship will inspire more interest, especially from those who are not in the job market. Poor salesmanship will have the opposite effect, attracting only those who are actively looking for work.

### Step Three: Screening Candidates

After making hundreds of calls to prospective candidates, the recruiter receives dozens of resumes from interested people. How does this stack of resumes get transformed into a short list of the very best candidates for the hiring manager to consider? It's done through an exhausting set of phone and (usually) in-person interviews.

The recruiter begins by doing a quick sort into "yes," "no," and "maybe" piles. Returning to our example, let's assume fifty people were interested enough to send resumes. The recruiter scans through them, spending a minute or so with each one. Most of them—somewhere from half to two-thirds—aren't close enough to the specification to warrant further time. Perhaps the candidate doesn't have enough years of experience, hasn't spent enough time in the fishing equipment industry, hasn't managed enough people, or has expertise in communications when the company really wants an expert in marketing strategy. Whatever the case, they go into the "no" pile, and the recruiter will call them back to let them know the company has candidates who are a better fit with its specification.

A smaller group—say, twelve to fifteen—is close enough to the specification to merit a phone interview. They go into the "yes" pile, and the recruiter contacts them to schedule a call. The phone interviews typically take between forty-five minutes and one and a half hours. More on this later.

Finally, the rest of the resumes go into the "maybe" file. These are potential candidates who are close to the specification but are missing one or two important qualifications. Since executive searches often take unanticipated twists and turns, it's wise to keep these potential candidates on the back burner. The recruiter will contact them to let them know there are other candidates who appear to be a better fit. However, the recruiter should also leave the door open to re-contacting these individuals later in the process, if necessary.

Now the recruiter has a short stack of qualified resumes, and he can begin in-depth telephone interviews. These phone interviews serve several purposes. First, they allow the recruiter to figure out whether there are any factors that would disqualify the candidate from consideration. Second, they enable the recruiter to explore the candidate's background in depth. Finally, and just as importantly, they give the candidate a chance to learn more, so he can determine whether he wants to invest more time exploring the opportunity.

We'll talk about what goes into a good interview in the next chapter, but it's worth briefly discussing disqualifying factors here. To put it simply, the recruiter needs to find out whether there are any issues that would make it difficult or impossible for the company to hire a candidate. These include compensation that's too high, stock options or deferred compensation that make it unlikely a candidate will leave his current employment, non-compete agreements, and an inability or unwillingness to relocate, if that's required.

It seems obvious that issues like these should be covered at the beginning of discussions, but you might be surprised to learn how often that doesn't happen. In the worst-case scenario, these questions are ignored until the hiring manager decides to extend an offer. Then he is shocked to discover that there is an impassable gulf between what he can afford to pay and the candidate's expectations, that relocation is suddenly out of the question, or that a previously unmentioned non-compete agreement makes hiring the candidate impossible. Untold hours of management time have been wasted on a candidate who was never viable, and the search goes back to square one. This situation is entirely avoidable, and a good recruiter will filter out candidates who cannot be hired before they ever reach the hiring manager.

The phone interviews dramatically narrow the field. From here, there are two options for narrowing the field further to a short list of finalists for presentation to the hiring manager.

One option—the preferable one, in my opinion—is for the recruiter to meet each of the remaining candidates face-to-face. That's what executive search consultants typically do. It's an important step, because it gives the recruiter an opportunity to assess the candidate's style, interpersonal skills, and potential for fit with the hiring manager and client company.

The second option is to skip face-to-face interviews with the recruiter and advance the best candidates directly to the hiring manager. This is more common when an in-house recruiter is conducting the search, but sometimes companies will ask an outside recruiter to do this, in an effort to save money on travel. The obvious disadvantage is that it is much harder for the recruiter to make a meaningful judgment about fit if she has not met the candidate in person.

When companies choose this approach, they usually believe they are saving time and money. Those savings are usually illusory. It's true that the hiring manager sees the first candidate slightly faster then he would otherwise, but the fact that he is meeting candidates who are less thoroughly screened will probably add time and cost to the process in the long run.

What about videoconferencing, you may ask. Some people view videoconferencing as an alternative to in-person meetings, but I have used it extensively and am not a fan. Video is a pale imitation of real life, and it can't begin to match what you'll learn about a candidate's presence and interpersonal skills when you're in the same room. In fact, given the choice between a phone call and a video conference, I'll take the phone call every time.

That completes our brief overview of identifying, contacting, and screening potential candidates. Now you know what's inside the executive search black box—hours of unglamorous work in the trenches. I hope I've made a compelling case for the necessity of using a recruiter, be it in-house or outside. We'll discuss those two options in some depth shortly.

But first, there may be an opportunity for you to bypass the need for a full-blown search by exploiting your personal network and those of your colleagues. Let's briefly look at how that works.

## Short-Circuiting Candidate Development: Networking

What if you could skip most of the candidate development described above? You'd save a lot of time, get a new executive in place faster, and perhaps even save money on recruiting fees. It sounds like fantasy, something that's too good to be true.

Yet the opportunity is quite real if you are willing to invest time in recruiting through your personal network. I know a number of CEOs who have made recruiting through their networks an art form. When they are successful, they short-circuit the laborious candidate development process, saving both time and money, and they end up with new hires who come highly recommended by people they trust.

If you haven't employed this tactic, you probably want to know more. There are a couple of prerequisites for success. First—and obviously—you need a strong network. If you are just beginning your career, or if you have worked at just one company, your network may not be wide enough to get you anywhere.

Second, you must be willing to put in some time. Although recruiting through your network (when successful) can be a big timesaver, it still requires significant effort and must be done by you personally, not someone you've deputized for the task. If you can't devote many hours to this, it's unlikely to produce results.

Are there any downsides? You bet. If you aren't careful, the lure of saving time can, ironically, turn into your greatest source of delay. I am often retained by hiring managers who have spent months canvassing their networks in vain before deciding to launch a professional search. The cost of the delay to the client's business, not to mention his sanity, is always many times my fee. Delays can be avoided by setting a time limit for networking, say two to four weeks, after which you will stop and launch a full-blown search. Without a deadline, it's easy for things to drag on, and then you'll have transformed the promise of a fast hire into lost weeks or months.

There's another risk to look out for, too. In the rush to fill an important position, it's tempting to take a trusted colleague's opinion of a candidate at face value and skimp on the usual due diligence. Perhaps interviews are less challenging, or maybe referencing is neglected. That's a terrible mistake. It's helpful to know that your friend Bob thinks highly of the candidate, but you have to form your own opinion. Make sure all of the candidates who are sourced through your network are put through the standard, thorough interviewing and vetting process. Don't give anyone a free pass.

Finally, if you fill a job through your network, by definition you are not looking at the entire pool of potential candidates. Maybe that's okay if the standard is "good enough," but if you're recruiting for a key position and need the best possible person for the job, your network may not deliver. A full-blown search is the only way to get a snapshot of the entire candidate pool, so you can feel confident you've looked at all available options.

## Options for Conducting a Search

If your network delivers a healthy slate of candidates, that's great news. However, the odds are it won't, and you will have to launch an all-out search. How is that done?

There are two options. The first, which is typically only available to those working at large companies, is to work with an internal talent acquisition group that has the ability to recruit at the executive level.

In recent years, companies that recognize the strategic importance of talent have put significant resources into building these organizations. Many employ outstanding people in the talent acquisition function, and some can recruit executives.

Recruiting from the inside is attractive in theory, but most companies don't have the people or organization to pull it off. Although strong talent acquisition organizations are more common than ever, they are still not ubiquitous, even at large companies. Further, most talent acquisition groups have not been built to recruit executives. The need for executive talent ebbs and flows, and the people who do it well are expensive, so building a group to recruit executives rarely makes economic sense. That's why it is so commonly outsourced.

If you have an internal talent acquisition partner who says he can help you, evaluate his capabilities carefully. What is the group's track record on similar projects? Are they appropriately staffed to put in the work required? Is the talent acquisition partner someone you trust and want to work with? If you decide to work with an insider, you should feel good about the answers to all of these questions.

What if you can't get help on the inside? If you don't have access to an appropriate internal resource, or you do but don't believe he can do the job, retaining an executive search consultant is the best option.

Retained search firms focus exclusively on recruiting senior-level people. There's no denying that the service is expensive—typically one-third of the new hire's first-year cash compensation—but when it is done well it is a great value, and the client enjoys a return that is many times the recruiting fee. In the short term, hiring a search consultant saves untold hours of the hiring manager's time. But it's the long-term payback that's most valuable: having the right person in a key executive position means the company's performance in the executive's area will far exceed that of a mediocre player. The best vice president of R&D will develop better products, the best vice president of sales will deliver more revenue, and so on. The quality of executive talent is directly related to company performance.

Unfortunately, executive search often fails to live up to its promise. Companies share some of the blame for this because they continue to hire non-performing executive search firms. In fact, many companies fail to track search firm performance at all. Why? Historically, executive search firms were hired based on relationships, and that's often still the case today. It's a quintessential old-boy (and old-girl) network, and decisions about what firms to retain are made at the country club as frequently as they are based on a careful analysis.

Making an informed decision that results in choosing the best executive search partner requires getting past superficial factors, and digging into each search consultant's capabilities, background, and method of working. When evaluating search firms, ask the following questions:

*Who Will Work on the Search If I Hire Your Firm?* Early on, find out whether the consultant at the meeting will work on the search. If the answer is yes, what will his role be? Specifically, will he make phone calls to present the opportunity to potential candidates, do phone and in-person interviews, write candidate assessments, and perform other critical tasks? If the answer is no, find out who will. Form an opinion about the person's ability to convince top candidates to consider the job.

*What Have You Done Recently in My Industry?* A consultant needs to understand the client's business well enough to present the opportunity to candidates in a knowledgeable way. Ask the consultant to name specific projects she has worked on in the industry. The consultant's personal experience is what matters, so be careful to distinguish between the consultant's work and that of the firm.

*Have You Worked on Searches in This Function?* Ask for specifics on projects for which the consultant was personally responsible. Try to get a sense of the consultant's understanding of the function and any special recruiting challenges.

*Do You Have Time to Give My Project the Attention and Focus It Needs?* Ask the consultant who will handle the assignment how many projects he is working on. Executive search consultants seldom turn down a project, even when they are very busy, so it is up to the client to form an opinion on whether a consultant has enough time to focus on a new search.

*If I Hire You, What Companies Will You Be Unable to Recruit From?* Ethical recruiting firms won't recruit from their clients. That means it's important to understand exactly which companies will be off-limits to the search. Search firms, especially the largest ones, are reluctant to admit off-limits issues. Be prepared to ask about specific companies that may be good sources of candidates, and don't settle for vague assurances.

*Are You Doing Any Similar Searches Right Now?* This question is an attempt to figure out whether the search firm has other projects that will compete for candidates. It is reasonable to assume that the larger the search firm, the greater the likelihood that the firm will be unable to show you candidates who have already been assigned to other clients. With the largest firms, it is almost a certainty.

*In What Percentage of Searches Is One of Your Candidates Hired?* If a consultant answers this question by citing the firm's completion rate, ask exactly what that means and dig into the underlying data. Hiring rates above 90 percent are usually not credible, simply because some searches are stopped when clients lose funding, suffer a business setback, or change strategies.

*How Will You Communicate with Me during the Search?* There should be a plan for regular communication with the client during the search. This could include regular teleconferences, meetings, written status reports, or all of the above. Most consultants will tailor the frequency and type of communications to the client's preferences.

*Who Can I Talk to About Your Work?* Obtain names of three clients who can speak to the specific consultant's work. Follow through and ask specific questions about their satisfaction with the search process and the end result. If possible, supplement the consultant's own references with others who can speak about his work.

## Summary

Identifying, attracting and screening candidates is a 4- to 8-week process that produces a group of 4 to 6 highly qualified finalists.

- Identifying candidates is easy thanks to online resources.
- The real work is attracting and screening prospective candidates. This requires hundreds of calls and many hours.
- A senior-level person who can interact with candidates as a peer must lead this process.
- Hiring managers do not have time to do this themselves; they must get help.
- There might be an internal resource capable of conducting the search, but that's rare.
- In most cases, the hiring manager needs to retain an executive search firm.
- Some hiring managers can bypass laborious candidate development by recruiting through their networks. Try it, but if it is not working, fall back quickly to a full outside search.

# Chapter 5

# Selling, Questioning, and Listening: The Art of the Interview

Mark Campbell is an expert in public speaking who teaches a class on communications to physicians and physician leaders at the Harvard School of Public Health.

Mark's students are graduates of the world's best universities and medical schools, and are employed at the most prestigious hospitals. This high-powered group of midcareer physicians has mastered almost everything related to their demanding jobs. Yet Mark's class is a perennial favorite, and his students engage the material with unusual energy and enthusiasm. Why is this so?

The answer is simple: they are hungry for Mark's instruction because public speaking is a skill that is not taught at universities and medical schools. For obvious reasons, medical education is focused on the diagnosis and treatment of patients. While this system produces physicians who have exceptionally high technical competence, it does not train them in the skills needed to chair a department or manage a hospital.

However, when called on to speak, physicians are expected to perform at a high level, and that's especially true for those who advance in hospital administration. They will be required to make high-stakes presentations that will determine the future course of their careers, and many of them feel unprepared. Success in an important presentation can mark a leader for the fast track—and conversely, a high-profile failure can destroy chances for advancement. That's why his students are so hungry for the material presented in Mark's class.

Executives in the business world face the same issues as Mark's students. They've never been taught public speaking, yet they are expected to do it well without training. It's an unreasonable expectation, like demanding that someone who's never ridden a unicycle hop on and ride it around the block.

There's another important "soft" skill that is not taught in school, and that's *interviewing*. It's the single most important part of candidate selection, so competence in interviewing is arguably the most important skill a businessperson can have. If you accept the proposition that hiring great people is a prerequisite for success in business—and almost everyone does—then great interviewing skills are a necessity.

Without the data gleaned from an effective interview, a hiring manager makes decisions in the dark. Sure, he'll get lucky and recruit some good people, but he'll also hire many bad ones. And unlike an important speech, where it's apparent right away if the speaker has bombed, it may take many months for an executive to realize he's hired the wrong person. Watching the career trajectory of an executive who is bad at interviewing is like watching a slow-motion train wreck.

One of the reasons interviewing is not taught is that it looks so simple on the surface. After all, people say to themselves, it's just talking with someone, and we do that all the time. But of course, it's much more than that. The interviewer must be prepared, must know what information he wishes to learn, and must know how to skillfully lead the conversation so it is as informative as possible.

Over my years as an executive search consultant, I've developed and refined my own interviewing style. This chapter outlines my approach. It's highly structured, yet flexible, and it's effective at unearthing the real story of the candidate's career trajectory and accomplishments. That's exactly the kind of information that hiring managers need in order to make better recruiting decisions.

## Learning the Candidate's Story

People understand one another through stories. Given a series of facts about someone, our instinct is to string them together in some sort of narrative.

Imagine you've never heard of Richard Branson, and a friend told you about an unusual British entrepreneur who'd started a string of spectacularly successful businesses, including a record retailer, an airline, a wireless phone carrier, and a space tourism company.

Wow, you'd say to yourself, who is that guy? What kind of person would even dare to found such a wide variety of businesses, and how on earth did he make them all successful? What's he like? Where does he get his drive and ambition? What makes him so successful? Without even thinking about it, you'd start building his story.

We do the same thing when meeting anyone new. Imagine a new person moves into your neighborhood and drops by to introduce herself. You might politely ask a series of questions about her background. Where did you live? What do you do for work? Do you have any kids? Where did you grow up? And so on. You're gathering information to build the story of your new neighbor in an effort to understand her better.

The same thing happens during an interview. Whether you are conscious of it or not, during an interview you're building a story about the candidate and her career. You're trying to understand her skills, achievements, motivations, personality, and other attributes so you can put them into a narrative that makes sense and explains who she is, how she got where she is today, and where she might go in the future.

Of course, building a story about anyone or anything is a highly subjective process. Anyone who's watched the evening news knows there are many ways to report the same set of facts. It all depends on the perspective of the person doing the reporting.

This holds true in the world of hiring as well. Naturally, the story you hear from the candidate about her skills, accomplishments, and background will put her in the best possible light. It will amplify her skills and achievements, and downplay her weaknesses and failures. In short, her version of the story will be a highly self-interested and overwhelmingly favorable presentation of the facts.

As the interviewer, you can't accept the candidate's narrative at face value. The interview is your opportunity to get past the candidate's version of her story and build a more objective and complete picture of her background. If you do a good job, you'll get answers to critically important questions. What did she accomplish, and why did it matter for her employer? What mistakes did she make along the way? What drove the major decisions in her work life? Why was she drawn to the companies where she worked and the jobs she held? Why did she change jobs? Answers to these questions and others will get you closer to an objective evaluation of her career.

Of course, getting straight answers to questions like these is easier said than done. Candidates will defend their version of the story like a fencer, meeting every one of your lunges with a skillful parry. That's why you must be prepared with a sound interviewing strategy, and determination to politely press the offensive until you are satisfied you've received answers to your questions.

## Before You Start: Verifying Education

There's one other simple thing to do before you begin meeting candidates face-to-face: verify their educational credentials.

Misrepresenting education isn't quite as common at the executive level as the press would have us believe, but it happens with some regularity. Stretching the truth or outright lying is common enough that I've made it a practice to verify every candidate's educational credentials before doing an in-person interview. Education seems to be a "gateway lie," and I want to weed those people out before my client and I invest time on them.

I learned this lesson the hard way. Early in my executive search career, I traveled to Minneapolis to meet a candidate for a search I was doing for a president of a manufacturing company. On paper the candidate was excellent, and he seemed strong in person, too. He had done his homework on the company, he was obviously very bright, and he had a high-energy style that I knew would be appealing to my client.

Yet my gut told me something wasn't right. When I returned to the office, I decided to verify his education and call some references. His education didn't check out—it was all a fabrication. Then I called his former boss, and when I described the candidate's claimed responsibilities and accomplishments, he was momentarily speechless. Finally he stammered, "He just didn't do that," in a voice that conveyed genuine shock and surprise. In hindsight, the candidate had all the traits of a sociopath, including high intelligence, great charm, and a total disregard for the truth.

I had dodged a bullet—the candidate had not met my client—but I'd still wasted plenty of my own time. I resolved that in the future, I would verify education before meeting anyone in person.

When I tell this story, many people ask, "But how do you verify education? Doesn't that take a lot of time?" No, it doesn't; verifying education is easy, and takes about five minutes. A simple call to the registrar's office at the school is usually all it takes. In some cases, the school will refer you to a third-party service that verifies education for a small fee. Five minutes is a small price to pay when measured against the many hours of management time that could be spent interviewing a candidate who's not truthful.

The nightmare scenario is a candidate who goes through many rounds of interviews, consuming hours upon hours of management time, and is then found to be a liar. It's embarrassing for everyone involved, but none more than the hiring manager, who takes the blame for wasting his colleagues' time and delaying the date of a critical new hire.

Even worse are those cases where no one ever checks, and the fraudulent candidate is hired. Every few months the *New York Times* or *Wall Street Journal* features a story on a prominent executive who's been caught lying about his credentials. In every case, someone failed in the basics of candidate due diligence.

Ending up in either situation will make you look very bad indeed. You can dramatically lower the possibility of that happening by verifying education early in the process.

## Planning for the Interview

Before the candidate walks in the door, you need to have a plan for how you will conduct the interviews. That includes defining who will be involved and what their roles will be.

Defining who will be involved in interviewing sounds simple, and it is, but it's easy and quite common to make mistakes. If key people are left out, they may not support your new hire, and that would set her up for failure. But if you include too many people, you'll be inviting input from individuals who don't have a stake in the process, and it will be much more difficult to achieve any kind of agreement. You'll create a giant, lumbering committee that slows everything down.

Who needs to be involved besides the hiring manager? Include only those people who have a genuine interest in the new hire. Everyone else should be excluded. For example, if you are recruiting a new vice president of manufacturing, the vice president of R&D and the CFO will work closely with the new executive and may want to be involved. Keep the core group as lean as possible. At the end of the process, you may include other people as a courtesy, if you wish. But they aren't part of the core decision-making group.

Of course, your boss (or one or two members of the board, if the board is your boss) may want to interview the finalist. Usually these interviews are a courtesy. Any of these individuals could exercise a veto, if they wished, but they will be reluctant to do so unless they believe you are headed off a cliff.

How should you structure the interviews themselves? I strongly recommend that the hiring manager interview candidates before involving anyone else. This gives you an opportunity to confirm that the candidate is indeed a realistic prospect. The cost of interviewing, in terms of management time, is quite high. Don't ask for your colleagues' valuable time unless you're sure you've got a viable candidate for them to interview. If the candidate is local, it will be easy for you to meet him in person before passing him on to others. If he's not, do a phone interview before you fly him in to meet with other members of the team.

How many rounds of interviews are necessary? Two is a minimum, and three is fairly typical—that includes round one with the hiring manager, round two with the core interviewing team, and round three for the courtesy interviews. In some cases a fourth interview makes sense.

More than four rounds starts to get ridiculous, and usually indicates that the hiring manager is too timid to make a decision. I've heard from many unfortunate candidates who were subjected to five, six, seven, or more rounds of interviews. If you do that, you'll be sowing the seeds of your own career's demise. Good candidates will run away, and those who remain will resent the poor treatment and your lack of professionalism. Further, your boss and peers will conclude (correctly) that you don't know what you're doing.

## The Roadmap

My approach to interviewing is simple: I lead the candidate through a highly structured discussion of every job in her career. This method takes considerably more time than less-rigorous approaches. The results are worth it, and the effort is modest in comparison to the time and cost required to undo a poor hire.

The premise for conducting interviews in this way is quite simple. I subscribe to the idea that past performance is the best predictor of future performance. If you believe that—and most people do—then hiring great people requires understanding what they have achieved in the past in great detail.

Some might object that there are exceptions to this rule. We've all heard stories of long shots who achieved great success after a string of ugly failures. But as a hiring manager, you're probably not looking for a long shot. You're looking for someone who has a high probability of succeeding in a job that is critical for your company's (and your own) success. Those people have a track record of achievement that suggests they can succeed in your organization, too.

I divide the interview into two sections: the candidate's questions and mine. These sections are by no means equal. My questions take about 80 percent of the interview, and the candidate's take about 20 percent.

Set the stage by making the candidate as comfortable as possible. Don't make the interview feel like an interrogation. A candidate who's uncomfortable will be on the defensive, and her measured answers to your questions won't be very revealing. If you put her at ease, she will be more forthcoming, and you'll learn more from the discussion.

Many people approach the interview as an adversarial process. They go out of their way to make candidates feel uncomfortable, usually because they believe that doing so will reveal something about how candidates respond to high-pressure situations.

I'm not a fan of this approach. High-pressure interviews have the effect of shutting down communication. The candidate's defenses go up, and the interviewer ends up learning very little. Further, many candidates will be so turned off by a "pressure interview" that they'll never come back. If you want to learn something from your interactions with candidates, and you want to keep the best people interested, don't take this path.

## Part One: The Candidate's Questions

There is no better sign of a good candidate than insightful questions. I ask the candidate to pose his questions first, for three reasons.

First, answering questions almost always provides another chance to sell the job and the company. Early in the interviewing process, candidates are still trying to figure out how interested they are in the job. Remember that you are both buyer and seller, and seize on any opportunities to reiterate why the job and the company are attractive.

Second, I want to deal with objections before they color the rest of our discussion. Often the candidate has one or more nagging doubts, and putting them to rest early makes the rest of the conversation far more positive. I don't want to go through a ninety-minute interview only to find out at the end that the candidate has a fundamental concern about the job that I could have handled much earlier.

Third, and most important, are the insights questions provide into the candidate. A candidate's questions show what she cares about, how smart she is, and how interested she is in the job. That's valuable information I can use later, when I pose my questions.

It will immediately become clear whether a candidate has done his homework. In all likelihood there is a wealth of information about your company online, and serious candidates will have studied it prior to the interview. If not, it may indicate that the candidate isn't very interested, or that he was just too lazy to prepare. Probe further to find out.

Questions also give insight into the candidate's values and working style. For example, a candidate for a position at a startup once asked me, "What kind of administrative support does this position have?" The question demonstrated that he didn't understand the resource constraints of startups. My answer was, "None. Everyone from the CEO down does his or her own administrative work. If you don't like the sound of that, this might not be the right position for you."

In another instance, a candidate for a regulatory affairs position at a medical device company asked unusually detailed and perceptive questions about the company's business performance and strategy. She had done her homework, but more importantly her insights demonstrated that she was one of the rare regulatory affairs professionals who understands and appreciates the big picture. My client was looking for a business-oriented regulatory executive, and this candidate's questions indicated she was one of them.

## Part Two: The Interviewer's Questions

After the candidate's questions, it's my turn. I care most about the candidate's recent experience—roughly the last ten years—so I start with the current job and work backward. This way I can dig deeply into the candidate's recent history and compress the discussion of older jobs, or schedule a follow-up if time runs short.

Thoroughly cover each position. Start by asking big-picture questions to establish the context in which the candidate worked, and then drill down into the details of the candidate's position and accomplishments. Although every interview is unique, all should cover these basic questions:

### Dates

Many resumes don't list months of employment, only years. Usually that's done to mask a gap in employment. Ask for these details if they haven't been provided, and when you find a gap, dig deeper to find out what happened. You need to understand the reason for each job change.

### What's the Business?

Ask the candidate to describe the business for which she works (or worked). If you're not familiar with the company, this provides detail that will enable you to place her work within a larger business context. If you know the company, you will usually learn more about its current situation. You will also learn a lot about the candidate's communication skills. A crisp and succinct answer, like "Acme is a $500M, privately held company that's the number-two manufacturer of electronics for small aircraft," is a good start. In contrast, a long-winded answer that starts with a detailed overview of

## NINE ESSENTIAL INTERVIEW QUESTIONS

1. When did you begin and end the job?

2. Tell me about the business so I can put your work in some context.

3. Why did you join the company?

4. How do you fit into the organization?

5. What were the challenges you faced when you joined?

6. Did you make changes to your team?

7. What did you accomplish?

8. How did you perform against your key metrics?

9. Why did you leave?

the aviation market for the last several decades demonstrates an inability to tailor an answer that's appropriate to the circumstances.

### Why Did You Join the Company?

You need to understand why the candidate thought joining each employer was a good career move. The answer to this question usually provides insight into her goals, values, and business savvy. When the candidate isn't being forthcoming, usually it's easy to tell. The answer doesn't quite make sense. When you suspect you're not getting a complete answer, keep following up until you're satisfied.

### Organization

Job titles can be misleading. A common title like *vice president of marketing* can mean very different things at different businesses. This is especially true at large companies with highly matrixed organizations that make it difficult to understand who is responsible for what.

I've found that the fastest way to understand a candidate's job, and how it relates to the overall business, is to ask him to verbally sketch the company organization and how he fits into it. To what position does he report? What reports to him? What positions are peers? This gives a clear picture of his responsibilities and how they relate to the rest of the company. Sometimes you'll discover that an individual with a very grandiose title doesn't have direct responsibility for anything. Or you may find out that someone with a relatively modest title has much more responsibility than you assumed.

### Situation

What was the situation when the candidate came on board? Was the company or the group in good shape, or were there problems? What were the top short- and long-term objectives?

These questions reveal a lot about how the candidate thinks and how well he communicates. A crisp answer that succinctly delineates the major challenges and how the candidate chose to tackle them is a promising sign; it indicates that the candidate is a smart, structured thinker who can communicate complexity in a simple way.

A long, rambling answer is red flag. It suggests that, even with the benefit of hindsight, the candidate doesn't have a handle on the problems he was facing, or is unable to communicate them.

### Team

Was the team in good shape when the candidate joined? Did he make changes? Why? What was the outcome?

The answers will tell you a lot about the candidate's approach to evaluating people, mentoring, managing, and whether or not he's comfortable making tough personnel decisions. Candidates who speak thoughtfully about their approach to hiring and mentoring people earn high marks. On the other hand, you would probably like to avoid those who are slow to fire weak performers or, on the other extreme, those who routinely turn over most of the team when they take on a new job.

## What Were Your Accomplishments, and Why Did They Matter to the Business?

This question is so obvious that every candidate should have a well-prepared answer. However, many do not.

A good answer goes something like this: "I did three things of which I'm especially proud. First, we were suffering from declining margins in our core product line. I proposed and got approval for a plan to cost-reduce the products. It took about two years to complete the work and introduce the new line, but when it was complete our gross margins rose by eight points. Second, . . ." Answers like this demonstrate clarity of thought and show awareness of how the individual's work contributed to the overall business.

There are many ways to answer this question poorly. Perhaps the most common is to provide a laundry list of responsibilities, rather than accomplishments. The inability of these candidates to connect their work to an improvement in their employer's circumstances suggests they just don't have an executive's mindset.

## Performance

Don't neglect to ask candidates about the performance metrics that are relevant to their function. How did the candidate perform versus plan? Versus the past? What impact—good or bad—did he have?

For salespeople, you need to know how they performed versus revenue targets. The relevant metrics for other functions are sometimes less clear-cut, and can be dependent on the particular circumstances and strategic goals of the business. For example, for marketing executives, the right metrics might be new product introductions, or growth in market share. For manufacturing executives, it might be improvements in gross margin, or a successful move to a new manufacturing facility.

## Why Did You Leave?

Make sure the explanation adds up. Euphemisms like "it was mutual" almost always mean the candidate was fired. Dig deeper and find out what happened.

Of course, being fired is not in and of itself a negative. Many of the world's most accomplished businesspeople were fired from one or more jobs. Understand what happened and what the candidate learned from the experience. Sometimes failure is the crucible that enables future successes.

As you're asking these questions, remember that the interview should feel like a conversation, not an interrogation. You're not following a rigid script, and at many points you will interject, ask for further explanation, ask follow-on questions, and so on. If you're doing a good job, you will learn new information that suggests new lines of questioning that weren't in your plan.

## Listening, Interrupting, and Asking Tough Questions

Listen carefully to what the candidate is telling you. More often than not, items of great importance will be communicated in subtle ways. Much of the critical communication will be nonverbal. If the candidate seems uncomfortable, or if you get a vague or incomplete answer, probe further.

Be aware of your own biases, because they will prevent you from picking up on important information. This is a particular risk if you're talking with a candidate you like. If you make up your mind too early, it's easy to miss red flags. Don't give anyone a free pass.

An interview is not polite conversation. By definition, it's imbalanced: you're asking questions, and the candidate is answering them. Ask questions, and then stop talking and listen. Interject when you want more detail. Don't allow yourself to behave like Charlie Rose, the television journalist who has become famous for talking more than his guests. You won't learn anything if you're doing all the talking.

What if the candidate is rambling? Should you interrupt to get her back on track? Sometimes candidates will talk on and on because they are filibustering in an attempt to avoid answering a question. If that's what's happening, I always interrupt. I want to nip that tactic in the bud and alert the candidate that this is an interview, not the floor of Congress.

What if the candidate launches into a monologue? For example, it's not uncommon to ask a simple question like, "Why did you join your current company?" and get a rambling ten-minute answer. When a candidate keeps talking on and on, I usually give him free rein because I want to see what happens. If he can't stay focused on answering the question, or if he talks endlessly, that's all I need to know. Perhaps he lacks poise, doesn't listen, or is a poor communicator. I don't need to waste time figuring it out, because they are all fatal flaws.

Many interviewers stumble because they are uncomfortable asking tough questions. They don't want to be impolite. After all, in normal social conversation we wouldn't ask, "Why did you get fired?" or "Why is your business performing poorly?" or "How much money did you make last year?"

If you are uncomfortable asking these questions, get over it. As the interviewer, you have a job to do, and it includes asking difficult and challenging

---

### Getting Through a Bad Interview

You sit down to interview a candidate, and in less than five minutes you know he's not a fit. Now what?

First of all, don't waste time beating yourself up. Even if you've run an excellent candidate screening process, situations like this will occasionally happen. Some people are a lot better in phone interviews than they are in person.

My father, John Travis, founded our recruiting firm and taught me the ropes. The first time I encountered this situation, I turned to him for advice.

"I just interviewed someone who is a terrible fit for my client," I told him. "What should I do in situations like that? It seems like such a waste of time to continue with the interview, but it would also be rude to end it too early."

He thought about it for a moment, and then gave me his usual wise answer.

"You're right," he said, "you can't just end the interview after five minutes. That would be rude, and it would be a bridge burner with the candidate. And if you did that often enough, you'd earn a reputation you don't want.

"When I'm in that situation, I try to find something positive that I can take away from the meeting. No matter to whom you're talking, you can always learn something from them that's interesting and maybe even useful. And who knows, maybe in the future you'll have a project for the candidate that's a better fit."

---

questions. You can take some comfort in knowing that the candidate expects you to ask them. In fact, not doing so reflects poorly on you, and the candidate will wonder why you don't have your act together.

## Judging "Fit"

Figuring out whether a candidate has the required experience is straightforward. But there's an equally important piece of the puzzle, and that's the candidate's compatibility with your company culture.

How can you tell whether the candidate can work effectively with others in the organization? That's what is often called by the vague term *fit*. It can be difficult to determine fit, because it requires us to assess personality traits that can't be directly measured. Yet it's so important that I like to say that fit trumps resume every time.

First of all, let's define what *fit* means in the context of hiring. It doesn't mean that you went to the same schools, have potential to be friends, have similar personal backgrounds, or share other traits that might make for compatibility in your personal life. When it comes to work, *fit* refers to four things:

- *Shared motivations.* Most work cultures are defined by a few dominant values. At a nonprofit, the motivation might be devotion to a cause. At a hedge fund, it might be making money. Imagine what would happen if you swapped them. The hedge fund executive, who wants to maximize income, would be exasperated with the world of nonprofits, where employees earn discounted salaries and take satisfaction from fulfilling a social mission. The nonprofit executive would be equally frustrated by the focus on making money at a hedge fund.
- *Shared work ethic.* Some companies encourage work/life balance. At others eighty-hour weeks are the norm. A person who wants to leave at five o'clock every day won't do well at a company where working evenings and weekends

## WHAT IS FIT?

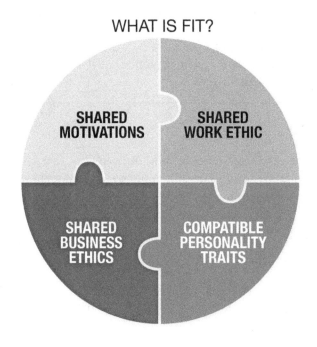

SHARED
MOTIVATIONS

SHARED
WORK ETHIC

SHARED
BUSINESS
ETHICS

COMPATIBLE
PERSONALITY
TRAITS

is expected. And the person who works eighty-hour weeks might be viewed as too intense or striving in a company that encourages balance.

- *Shared business ethics.* Companies must obey the law, but beyond that there are widely varying opinions on what constitutes good business ethics. One man's hard-nosed decision could be another's unethical one. For example, an executive who's proud he's never laid anyone off would not feel good about working for "Chainsaw" Al Dunlap, who gained renown as a ruthless job-cutter. And Chainsaw Al would probably view the executive who is proud of never laying off employees as weak and hopelessly sentimental.

---

### How to Tell People They Won't Get the Job

The competition for an executive position has only one winner. Everyone else ends up disappointed.

Surprisingly, making a simple phone call to tell a candidate she didn't get the job is something that many otherwise-tough executives try hard to avoid. In fact, one of the most common complaints I hear from job seekers is that they go through one or more rounds of interviews with a company, then never hear from them again.

So let me propose a simple ground rule—Get back to candidates promptly once you have decided they will not win the job. This is common courtesy, but if that's not good enough for you, it's also your business interest. If you treat people poorly on a consistent basis, you will earn a reputation as a company (or individual) to avoid.

How do you deliver that bad news in a kind way? You don't have to be too specific, but you must be direct. I'll commonly say something like, "The company has decided to pursue other candidates," or, "They're going in another direction." If I can provide helpful feedback (and if I believe the candidate can accept it without argument), I'll provide it.

I always end these conversations by thanking the candidate for taking time to explore the opportunity. I also tell them I'm glad we've met (if we've not met before), and that I hope I will have other projects to talk with them about in the future. And I mean it.

Whatever industry you're in, it's a smaller world than you might think. There is no upside to burning a bridge. Treating people as you would wish to be treated is the right thing to do, and may also pay off in unexpected ways in the future.

- *Compatible personality traits.* Companies have a personality that can be usually be boiled down to a set of must-have traits. For example, at one of my clients, the most important traits are high intelligence, commitment to working as part of a team, and highly evolved social skills. People who lack intellectual horsepower, have big egos, or are introverts simply don't make it there.

Judging fit requires a sort of corporate self-knowledge; that is, you need conscious awareness of what personal characteristics are good predictors of success in your company. Without this, discussions about fit quickly devolve into vague conversations about which candidates the interviewers liked and did not like.

Even armed with knowledge of what makes for a good fit, this remains an area where you have to use your intuition—defined as the unconscious application of expertise. There's no simple litmus test that will give you a yes or no answer. While you're talking with the candidate, you'll get a feel for the person and whether or not he has the characteristics you're looking for.

Judging fit is an art. Sometimes it's obvious, but more often it's a tough call. For me, becoming a good judge of fit came only after many years of experience. I think it's that way for most people. The good news for those who don't have a lot of experience is that you can get better quickly if you think about fit in a conscious and structured way.

## Summary

- Define who will be involved in interviewing. Include only those people who have a stake in the new hire. If you include too many people everything will slow down.
- Before you meet anyone, make sure you or your recruiting partner has verified educational credentials.
- If you make the candidate comfortable he will be more forthcoming. Pressure interviews never work.
- Lead the candidate through a structured discussion of her career and accomplishments using the guide in this chapter.

# Chapter 6

# Common Problems (And How to Fix Them)

In business, things rarely go exactly as planned. Reality is never as elegant as the beautiful flowchart outlined in your business plan—it's often quite messy. This is also true of recruiting. If you want your recruiting project to succeed, you have to be ready for anything.

Dealing with unforeseen obstacles is such an essential business skill that you could say the art of management is dealing with the unexpected. Execution requires grappling with a business world that is inherently turbulent, marred both by the obstacles thrown up by external forces and by those we inadvertently create for ourselves. A great manager, like a martial artist, fights off the kicks and punches that reality throws at him and persists until he wins.

Sometimes, we're knocked off course by an external event. The market crash of late 2008 is an example of an external event that had a heavy and universal impact on business. Very few people saw the meltdown coming, and business leaders were forced to rapidly adapt to a new reality with many unknowns. They scuttled their old plans and created new ones on the fly, all while the global economy crumbled and each day brought frightening new developments.

Most external problems are a lot less dramatic than the financial crisis. Perhaps a vendor suddenly stops making a single source component, putting production of an important product in jeopardy, or a customer goes out of business, taking with it a large piece of the year's sales forecast.

Then there are obstacles we create for ourselves through poor planning and lack of foresight. Maybe it takes longer than planned to develop a new product, or the cost of goods can't be reduced to the point that was forecast. Or perhaps there are delays bringing a new manufacturing plant online, jeopardizing margins, or problems in sales lead to lower-than-forecasted revenues. These are the kinds of problems business leaders tackle every day.

## Managing Recruiting Problems

Recruiting is not immune. I guarantee that you will run into problems when recruiting, just as you will in every other aspect of your business. You can work diligently, following all of the instructions laid out in this book, and things will still go wrong. Some obstacles will come from the outside, and others will originate in your own accidental oversight.

The first step in overcoming problems is recognizing they will happen. Awareness that you will run into obstacles makes it much easier to spot them. And when you recognize a developing problem early, you can take action before it threatens the success of your recruiting project.

What kinds of things can go wrong? Everything you can imagine and then some. I've been an executive search consultant for eighteen years, and every time I congratulate myself for having seen it all, I run into something entirely new. Here's an example.

Some years ago I was recruiting a vice president of marketing for a fast-growing, publicly held medical device firm. After a smooth and uneventful search, the company decided to extend an offer. The candidate they selected was smart and had all the right skills. In addition, she had a personal style that promised to be highly compatible with the company's culture. She accepted the offer, and since it was the end of the year, both parties agreed to set a start date that was a couple of months away so she could collect her year-end bonus before starting the new job.

Everything proceeded according to plan. The candidate received her bonus and gave notice to her employer. Although I never consider a search done until the new candidate is seated at her desk, I confess to having no concerns about this project. I was quite certain it was a done deal.

Early one morning about a week before the candidate's start date, I settled into my office and checked the business headlines. That's when I learned my client had been acquired. The news woke me up fast.

I never saw it coming, but I should have. Their growth rate was exceptional—far higher than the industry—and they made an attractive acquisition target. The company got a huge premium on its stock price, but even more importantly there was no overlap with the acquirer's business. In fact, the acquirer wanted them to continue operating exactly as they had in the past. There would be no job cuts, no painful integration into the mother company, and no disruptive departures of executives. Things would continue exactly as before; the only difference would be ownership.

The candidate didn't share that rosy view of the deal. She was understandably upset. She'd resigned a comfortable position to run marketing at an independent public company, and to her it felt like bait and switch. Further, she was skeptical about the acquirer's stated intention to leave the business alone. Her skepticism was quite reasonable: most acquisitions begin with positive talk, and then get messy when the acquirer begins to integrate its new division, or key executives move on.

The client and I did everything we could think of to convince her to stay the course and join the company. Yet in the end, despite all of our efforts, she couldn't overcome her concerns and rescinded her acceptance. We were back to square one. There was nothing to do but shrug off the setback and get back to work. The search had a happy ending when my client hired a different, equally outstanding candidate, but we had lost several months of valuable time.

That story is unusual, and it's unlikely you will encounter a similar situation. However, there are a handful of problems that are common, and if you do enough recruiting, you will encounter them over and over again. Learning to recognize them and take corrective action is a critical skill.

This chapter describes the six most common problems you will encounter when recruiting executives. It will help you to identify them and take corrective action while you can still get the search back on track.

## THE SIX MOST COMMON PROBLEMS

1 WE DON'T LIKE ANY OF THE CANDIDATES

2 THE CANDIDATES WE LIKE ARE TOO EXPENSIVE

3 NO ONE IS INTERESTED

4 CANDIDATES ARE INITIALLY INTERESTED, BUT THEY'RE DROPPING OUT

5 MY BOSS (OR THE BOARD) SHOT DOWN MY CHOICE

6 EVERYTHING IS GOING TOO SLOW

## Problem 1: We Don't Like Any of the Candidates

Imagine the following situation. You are six weeks into the search for a new executive. You've interviewed half a dozen candidates, and you don't like any of them. Things are definitely not going to plan—you had hoped to be zeroing in on one or two finalists after half a dozen interviews, and instead you haven't gotten out of the starting blocks. What's wrong?

Most executives will recognize this situation. It's a common problem that I like to call the "Goldilocks search." This candidate is too hot, that one is too cold, and no one is ever just right. What's happening?

A fashionable explanation, at least as I write this, is that there's a talent shortage. The popular business press generates a constant stream of stories about the alleged talent shortage that support this conclusion.

I don't believe there's a talent shortage. Sure, there are situations (usually involving highly specialized technical skills) where a specific type of talent is in short supply, and geographies (like Silicon Valley) where there's a chronic shortage of good people. But the idea that there is a general shortage of talent is laughable. If you're not finding candidates and blame the problem on a non-existent talent shortage, you will never identify the real issue or get back on track.

What could the real causes be? There are four possibilities.

### *Your Recruiter Is on the Wrong Track*

Let's start with the individual who is supporting your recruiting effort. It's possible he is not doing a good job. There are many ways a recruiter can go wrong.

Start with the most fundamental question: is your recruiter putting in enough time to get the job done? If you are working with an inside resource, there's an excellent chance there's too much on his plate. Many companies chronically underfund human resources and then dump an unrealistic workload onto recruiting professionals.

Having too many projects, however, is not a problem only with HR departments. Outside recruiters are commonly overcommitted, too. Usually they are working within a partnership that demands a high level of billings, and that gives individual recruiters a strong incentive to take on more work than they can realistically handle. There's a point at which an executive search consultant is juggling so many projects that he simply can't deliver high-quality work.

How can you tell whether you're getting enough attention? If you're working with a competent partner, you should receive regular updates on progress without asking for them. If you need to chase the recruiter for status, or if you sense there's little activity, there may be a problem. Talk with the recruiter and express your concerns. Ask questions to determine whether your project is getting enough time. If it's not, make it clear that you expect more, and if necessary go up the chain of command to make sure you get it.

There's another possibility: maybe the recruiter supporting you is just not very good. Does he have the smarts and business savvy to present the job opportunity to candidates in a compelling way, and to assess them in a way that's insightful and helpful? If not, more attention from the recruiter won't help; you need to switch horses. Explore ways to remedy the situation with HR leadership or with management of the recruiting firm.

It's relatively easy to diagnose a problem with your recruiter. The other potential problems are more difficult to identify because they originate with you, and require you to look in the mirror and recognize your own mistakes.

### You Don't Really Know What You're Looking For

Remember my story of failed Christmas shopping trips as a young man? I thought I knew what I was looking for, but I didn't. As a result, I wasted a lot of time and was never happy with the results.

No doubt you went to the trouble of drafting a detailed job description and candidate specification. That should mean you have this issue under control, but if you are interviewing many candidates and don't like any of them, it's worth re-examining.

Think about the candidates you've seen. Why don't they measure up? Are they falling short in areas that are called out in your written specification, or is it something else? Has the process of interviewing people caused you to rethink parts of the candidate specification? If so, does your recruiter know about the change in requirements?

Sometimes it helps to talk this through with a trusted colleague or advisor, since you may be dealing with a blind spot that will be difficult to uncover on your own. Sit down with a third party to discuss the issue. If you discover areas where the candidate specification has been vague or unclear, correct the oversight. Then, make sure to communicate your thoughts to the recruiter who is supporting you and to colleagues who are involved in the hiring process.

## You're Afraid of Making a Mistake

No one is perfect. If you are expecting the perfect candidate to walk in the door, one whom you can hire with no risk, you are in for a long wait.

If you find yourself rejecting candidates because they aren't perfect, ask yourself this question: Are you paralyzed by the fear of making a mistake? This happens when the hiring manager, faced with the responsibility of recruiting a high-profile new executive, get so hung up on the risk of making a mistake that he finds himself unable to hire anyone. If that sounds familiar, take comfort in knowing that this is a common problem.

It's exceptionally rare to find a candidate who meets every single item on a hiring manager's wish list. Each candidate comes with his or her own set of strengths and weaknesses relative to the specification. Hiring an executive is an exercise in understanding each candidate's positives and negatives in the context of the job you're trying to fill, and then choosing the one who offers the best set of trade-offs.

Many years ago—so many that the statute of limitations has now expired, and I can tell the story—I worked with a client who was afraid to make a decision. She was the owner of a very successful consulting firm, and she needed to recruit a leader for the company's most important practice area. The stakes were high. While it's a given that every executive hire is critical, that's especially true at small companies, where one individual can profoundly impact every aspect of operations. In short, the potential upside of making a great hire was exciting, but getting it wrong would be a disaster. As an owner, my client understood the stakes far better than most hiring managers, because she was spending her own money.

Further complicating matters, the owner did not have a lot of experience hiring people at this level. She had only done it three or four times in the history of the company. Her track record was well above average, but the last senior executive she'd brought into the company had not lasted long. That recent disappointment, along with knowledge of the importance of the recruiting task, made her especially cautious.

The search got off to a fast start, and I presented a strong group of candidates. One of the very first (I'll call him Fred) stood out because of his strong resume and engaging, extroverted personality. The combination of technical knowledge and great people skills was very rare in my client's field, and perfectly suited for the position she was trying to fill. I thought I'd hit the bull's-eye.

My client liked him too, but almost as soon as she expressed those positive thoughts, she began to question her own judgment. What if Fred's experience was insufficient? What if his contacts weren't good? And so on and so on. Within minutes she had tied herself up in knots of self-doubt. In the end, she found many small reasons not to hire him. We agreed to put Fred on the back burner while the client evaluated other candidates.

We kept looking. I presented many more talented people, some with far more years of experience than Fred. But for a variety of reasons, none of them made the grade.

After several months we went back to Fred, and with some anxiety my client agreed to proceed toward making him an offer. Yet she remained torn, and asked whether we could give Fred a personality test that might confirm the decision to hire him. I gently explained it was unlikely a test would shed any light on the situation. She would have to make a decision based on the information at hand and her own instincts.

My client hired Fred, and he proved to have a gift for consulting. In short order, he transformed the business. My client was delighted, but now she had a new worry: how could she retain Fred for the long haul? She set to work building additional long-term incentives to keep him at the company.

My client's story had a happy ending, but that's not always the case in these situations. To my client's credit, she made the leap of faith and hired someone.

Indeed, hiring anyone involves a leap of faith. Business leaders are human beings, and all of us have flaws. Further, as hiring managers we cannot see the future; we can only evaluate a candidate's past performance and hope that a strong track record will continue.

Don't allow yourself to be paralyzed by the fear of making a mistake. If you wait for a risk-free candidate, you will be waiting forever. There are always unknowns, and no candidate is perfect. Your job is to make the best choice possible given the information at hand. If you run a disciplined process such as the one outlined in this book, you will minimize the risk of making a bad hire.

If this is your problem, think hard about why you are so scared of failure. Talking with trusted colleagues about the situation and asking for their advice might help you to break through the impasse.

### There Are Too Many Cooks in the Kitchen

As noted in the last chapter, you should involve others in the hiring process, but including too many people will slow everything down.

I advise including only those people who have a genuine interest in the new hire, and excluding everyone else. That keeps the size of the core interviewing group manageable and limits involvement to those who have a serious stake in hiring the right person. The right number is usually two to four people, including the hiring manager.

Yet I have seen situations where the hiring manager wanted a dozen or more people involved in interviewing. This creates a host of problems that I will outline below. But first, why would any hiring manager want to involve so many people?

In my experience, hiring managers get too many people involved when they are overly concerned about building consensus. I am not talking about the normal consensus-building that executives need to achieve with colleagues and staff. I'm talking about a dysfunctional inability to act without the approval of a broad range of colleagues.

This is always a symptom of a deeper problem. Usually, it means the hiring manager is unsure of his ability to make the right choice, or he feels insecure about his position in the company. Whatever the root cause, he is terrified of disapproval. You might say that involving too many people is a way to abdicate responsibility for making a decision, instead turning it over to a committee.

Three bad things happen when too many people are involved in interviewing. First, logistics become a nightmare. Scheduling busy executives is hard, and it becomes exponentially more difficult as the number of people to be scheduled goes up. So scheduling slows everything down.

Second, candidates come away with a poor impression of the company. It's not uncommon for candidates to be interviewed by people who know very little about the position to be filled or what the hiring manager is seeking. Because these interviewers have little self-interest in the new hire, they prepare poorly. I've seen many instances where they did not even bother to read the candidate's resume. Great candidates immediately understand that these meetings are a waste of time for everyone involved.

Finally, it is difficult to achieve consensus with a large group. And since the hiring managers who create these large interviewing groups are obsessed with achieving consensus, searches go on forever. The hiring manager ends up rejecting good candidates because they did not win a 100 percent approval rating from the enormous interviewing panel.

If this is your problem, the fix is relatively easy. You simply need to cut back on the number of interviewers. Identify the few people who have a stake in the new hire and exclude everyone else.

## Problem 2: The Candidates We Like Are Too Expensive

Of all the problems discussed in this chapter, this one is the easiest to identify. It has one very concrete symptom: The candidates you like best cost more than the company is willing to pay. Your candidate specification describes a Bentley, but your budget will only buy a Chevrolet. What should you do?

One approach that won't work is hoping to find a bargain. Hope, as they say, is not a strategy. It's possible that someone, somewhere has a Bentley gathering dust in a barn, and that they'll part with it for the price of a Chevrolet because they don't know its true value. Maybe it's out there, and maybe you will find it, but going down that path requires unlimited time and a lifetime's worth of luck. There's an overwhelming likelihood of failure. Do you want to stake your success on a long shot like that?

What are some realistic ways to get things back on track?

One option is to raise your budget. In many cases this is not possible, due to business realities or company compensation policies.

Even if you can increase the budget, that doesn't mean you should do it. Pushing the limits of what you can afford has many downsides. First, it doesn't leave much room for future merit increases if the new hire does a good job. Second, paying someone compensation that is at the edge of your comfort zone can have the unintended effect of setting her up for failure. Anything less than superhuman performance may leave you feeling like you're not getting your money's worth. Think about the major-league baseball teams that hire star players for outlandish pay, and then feel embittered if the player doesn't set new records each year.

A second (and usually more palatable) option is to relax the candidate specification so it includes people you can hire within your budget. Of course, this will require making trade-offs. Maybe you won't get as many years of experience as you would like, or perhaps you'll end up with a seasoned utility player who's not a superstar but can get the job done. Decide what trade-offs make sense, then get back to work and hire someone.

There's a third option, and that's to restructure the function or department so you can get things done with affordable talent. There are many ways to skin a cat, and there are many ways to organize work so it can be done in an efficient and effective manner. Get creative and see whether you can think of an alternative way to structure your group with affordable people.

## Problem 3: Candidates Aren't Interested

What if many candidates are presented with the opportunity, but no one is interested?

When candidates aren't interested, it's like having a product that isn't selling. Hiring managers must act quickly to understand why. Is the business attractive? Is the opportunity being effectively sold? Are sights set too high? Let's take these possibilities one at a time.

### Is the Business Attractive?

Let's start with the business. Does it have any notable reputational problems? It's unlikely this will be the case, but if you work for today's equivalent of Enron or Tyco, or your last CEO was just indicted, you face a special challenge. Many candidates, perhaps most of them, will shut you out before you can even deliver your message.

You'll face similar resistance, though perhaps less severe, if there are other business problems. Maybe revenues are on a well-publicized downward slide, the company is rumored to be an acquisition target, or the government has initiated a high-profile enforcement action due to some real or perceived misdeed. Whatever the reason, candidates wonder whether they'd be signing up for a cruise on the *Titanic*.

Approach this problem like a good salesperson. You can't do anything about the shortcomings of the situation, but you can identify and highlight the positives. (And there must be positives or you wouldn't be there, right?)

Usually the same factors that are turning away candidates can be flipped on their heads and turned into positives. For example:

- *Revenues have been in a decline.* We need a marketing executive who can craft and execute a product strategy to reverse that trend.
- *The FDA shut down our manufacturing facility.* We've made mistakes and are committed to turning things around. We need a leader who can design and implement a new quality system.
- *The misdeeds of our old management team caused us to lose trust on Wall Street.* We need new leadership that can remake our culture and re-establish trust with our investors and business partners.

Of course, the examples above assume that your company recognizes its problems and sincerely wants to do something about them. If that is true, you're offering an opportunity to turn around a function or a business, and many candidates will find that to be very attractive.

If the company is on a downward trajectory and there's no mandate for change, your job will be a lot more difficult. You still must identify the positive attributes of the company and the job opportunity, but your message will be much weaker. You'll have to commit yourself to a tough search and grind it out. In addition, you may need to resign yourself to the fact that the job simply is not very attractive, and you may not be able to recruit the quality of candidate you want.

### Is the Opportunity Being Effectively Sold?

If candidates are not interested, it's also possible that whomever is contacting candidates is doing a poor job selling the opportunity.

Is someone competent and credible making the introductory calls to candidates? A typical executive search requires hundreds of phone calls. Making the frontline calls is a laborious and time-consuming process that is often assigned to junior recruiters who don't have the skill or business knowledge to make a credible presentation to candidates.

Every executive I know has a story about being contacted by a recruiter who was so transparently junior that his message was dismissed before it could be delivered. You've probably received many of those calls yourself. If you determine this is the problem, insist on a change in staffing to fix it.

If that's not the issue, review the "pitch" your recruiter is using with candidates. Recruiters don't have long to pique a candidate's interest, so the message must be crisp and compelling. If it's not, or if it doesn't present the company and the job in an effective way, fix it.

### Are Sights Set Too High?

There's a third reason candidates may not be showing interest, and that's if you're targeting people who are just too senior to be interested in the job you're trying to fill.

This is a fairly common problem, and it can be hard to diagnose. Most of us drink a healthy dose of our own Kool-Aid and have a highly biased view of our own company and its prospects.

I'm reminded of a friend who, years ago, worked for one of the most desirable employers in the country. Let's call them Awesome Corporation.

My friend was building a new business intelligence organization and wanted to recruit top performers from leading consulting firms. Because the company was Awesome Corporation, it wasn't hard to bring people to the table.

But my friend couldn't close them. In fact, he made three offers that were rejected. The people he wanted to hire were in great demand, and the positions he had on offer were a lateral move for them. In the end, the candidates took positions at other companies where they would enjoy more responsibility.

My friend believed that Awesome Corporation was such a magnet that top performers would jump at the chance to join, even for jobs that didn't represent an upward move. He learned the hard way that he'd overplayed his hand. He eventually refocused on candidates who would want the job, but by then he'd lost a lot of time and endured the humiliation of a string of rejections.

If you're worried you may have fallen into the same trap, it can be tough to figure this out by talking with work colleagues. After all, you probably share the same biases. Instead, talk with one or more trusted colleagues from outside the company who can give you an objective take on the situation. If you find that your expectations are unrealistic, adjust them.

## Problem 4: Lots of Candidates Are Interested . . . Until They Meet Us

The search appears to be off to a very promising start. High-quality candidates are interested, and they seem to be enthusiastic before they come in to interview. But then something goes wrong. After one or two meetings a high percentage of them drop out. What's going on?

There are a few possibilities. It could be that the company and its prospects are turning off candidates. That's unlikely, however, because they have already been through one or more phone interviews and had ample time to learn the basics about the firm.

A second possibility is candidates are hearing different stories about the job or the business plan from different interviewers. When dissonance is severe, it gives candidates the uncomfortable sense that you don't have your act together. If this is the problem, make a diagnosis. Sometimes (though not very often) it's a simple matter of poor communication among interviewers. That can usually be corrected with a meeting to get everyone back on the same page.

But it's more likely that candidates are picking up on important differences in the vision for the job, and that's a matter that isn't nearly as easy to resolve. You need to identify the areas of disagreement and arrive at some consensus before you can move forward. If you don't, people will continue to walk away.

A third possibility, and the most likely one, is that the problem is you. Poor listening, arrogance, and other forms of disrespect are turning candidates off, and they simply can't see themselves working for you. They say to themselves, "That may be a great position, but I can't work for that guy. If he's like this during the interview, when he's on his best behavior, it's only going to get worse if I take the job."

It's not easy to fix this problem—and most people who have it aren't interested in fixing it. If you're the exception, you need to solicit honest, hard feedback from trusted colleagues and be willing to listen to it. If you want to excel at recruiting (or anything else, for that matter) you need to be able to look into the mirror, see your flaws, and then take steps to improve.

## Problem 5: My Boss Shot Down My Choice

You've come up with a great candidate. But after your candidate meets your boss, a process you hoped would be a formality, she's vetoed your choice. What happened?

One possibility is that you failed to involve your boss earlier in the process. Now, when you thought you were nearly done, you discover she doesn't agree with you on the search's direction. If this is what's happened, you need to take a step back, listen to your boss's feedback, and come to an understanding before you get back to interviewing candidates.

If you report to the board of directors, it's quite possible that board members don't agree with one other. This is a difficult problem to manage, especially in venture-backed companies where board members (who are also investors) can have conflicting objectives. To get back on track, you have to drive them toward consensus. Make sure they know that nothing will move forward until they resolve their differences. Of course, it's easy to prescribe this solution but much harder to make it happen, especially if the board has deteriorated to the point of severe dysfunction.

## Problem 6: The Process Is Too Slow

Things are moving at a glacial pace. At this rate, you'll never make your target date for having the new hire on board.

It's possible that your HR support or recruiter doesn't share your sense of urgency. If that's the problem, make it clear you're not happy and demand more of their mindshare. If that doesn't work, get others to support you.

It's just as possible, however, that things are moving slowly because you haven't made hiring a priority. Perhaps you are not providing substantive and timely feedback on candidates. Or maybe you and other interviewers are not easy to schedule for interviews. All of the above may be true.

If you want hiring to move quickly, it must be at the top of your to-do list. Executives universally profess that building a great team is their most important task, but it's another thing to follow though, especially when there are dozens of other things competing for your time. Because making a new hire is a months-long process, it's easy to put off recruiting tasks when other urgent matters arise. Don't let that happen. If you need an incentive, imagine how much additional time you'll have each day after the new executive comes onboard.

## Summary

- Expect to encounter large and small problems. They happen even in the best-run recruiting processes.
- When you sense that something is going wrong, act quickly to make a diagnosis.
- Use this chapter as a guide to diagnosing the most common problems:
  - We don't like any of the candidates.
  - The candidates we like are too expensive.
  - No one is interested.
  - Candidates are initially interested, but they're dropping out.
  - My boss (or the board) shot down my choice.
  - Everything is going too slowly.
- Take action to fix things and get back on track. Most problems can be easily addressed, but if you let them fester they will imperil the success of the search.

Chapter 7

# How to Get Meaningful References

Imagine you could buy a magic wand that had the power to help avoid costly hiring mistakes. No matter what you did wrong, no matter what novice mistake you made along the way, the magic wand would get you back on track before you made an offer to someone who was doomed to fail.

What if it had another power, too? In addition to helping you avoid bad hires, the wand could give you deep insight into those you do hire. The knowledge would enable you to be a more effective manager, and help you make your new executives more successful.

You would probably pay a lot for that magic wand. But I have good news: it's free. The wand is more commonly known by another name—references. All you have to do is put in the time and effort to check them.

That's the catch; most people don't check references in a serious way. They don't approach references with an open mind, they don't probe, and they don't talk to enough people.

It's said that if exercise came in a pill, it would be the greatest blockbuster drug ever because of its far-reaching positive effects. Yet despite the evidence, most people don't exercise because it requires discipline, hard work, and time. There's a parallel with referencing. The benefits are obvious, but many people don't bother doing them right.

It's no exaggeration to say that referencing is the most underutilized tool in the hiring manager's arsenal. If you take nothing from this book but a commitment to check references in a more serious way, you will dramatically improve the quality of the people you hire.

For too many hiring managers, references are a formality to be conducted after a decision has already been made. After a long and grueling search for the right candidate, managers are understandably tired and impatient. They want to wrap things up and get the new executive on board. Whether they realize it or not, they enter the referencing process with a closed mind and are unwilling to hear or accept feedback that conflicts with their pre-conceived ideas.

I'm a big fan of the *New York Times'* wonderful column "Corner Office." It's a series of interviews with CEOs, and it's always enlightening. One of the profiled executives beautifully summarized the importance of references:

> I've interviewed tons of people and I've got a decent track record, but not great. I'm very self-aware about the fact that I'm not a perfect interviewer . . . I rely about 20 percent on my interview and the interviews my colleagues do with the person, and 80 percent on references. I'll find people we know in common and check what it was like to work with the person I'm interviewing. The truth comes out and that's when you get the real story.[1]

References, in other words, will help you to make better decisions, and that's especially true if you are not very good at interviewing or don't trust your own judgment. If you're good at doing references, you can get away with a lot of other mistakes. References will save you from yourself.

Here's an example of what can happen when references are neglected. The CEO of a mid-sized private company called me to discuss the search for a vice president. He had just fired the incumbent, who had been in place less than one month. Her poor people skills and desire to make big changes before she understood the company's operations made her continued employment impossible.

The CEO, obviously, had made a major mistake. He was rattled by the experience and didn't understand where he had gone wrong. He told me, "I don't know how she could have been so different from her references. All three of them were excellent."

That was all I needed to know. It was no wonder he had not uncovered any negative: he had spoken to only three people, and since he'd already sold himself on the candidate, they were undoubtedly superficial conversations. The candidate's problems weren't subtle, and even a cursory discussion should have turned them up.

The CEO hadn't begun to scratch the surface of proper due diligence. It was a hard and embarrassing lesson. I'm not sure he learned anything from his mistake, but the rest of us can.

## Why References Matter

Let's pause for a moment to review the purpose of references. There's more to it than you might imagine.

Why are references so important? Consider that everything you learn in an interview comes from the candidate, and as such it's inherently one-dimensional and self-interested. The candidate is selling, and he wants you to see only the most flattering aspects of his background.

You have to get past the flawless portrait he's painting. To develop a deeper and more nuanced portrait of the candidate as a worker and a person, you must fill out the picture with third-party testimony. References provide a unique opportunity to learn about candidates from a wide variety of former bosses, peers, and subordinates.

When you think about it, we ask for references all the time. For example, when buying a new car, I talk with the salesperson, take it for a test drive, and read reviews. Before making a decision, however, I'll talk with friends and acquaintances who own the same vehicle. Their observations are always insightful and go far beyond the self-interested patter of the salespeople. I give owners' opinions a lot of weight, and more than once they've saved me from a bad decision.

We do the same thing with restaurants, travel destinations, and other products. In fact, it's amusing and disturbing to realize that many people do more referencing on these relatively minor matters than they do when making a critical new hire.

What kinds of information can references provide about a candidate? Most people think of references as a search for reasons *not* to hire someone. It's true that sometimes referencing uncovers a fatal flaw that scuttles a candidacy. This is unusual, but when it happens it averts disaster and saves the hiring company time, money, disruption, and embarrassment. It also enables the hiring manager to avoid a potentially career-limiting mistake.

Referencing, however, is much more than that. In the vast majority of cases there are no fatal flaws to be found, but the hiring manager still gets valuable information.

First, referencing helps hiring managers feel confident in their choice. The effects of this confidence are subtle but important. Every new employee experiences bumps in the road as she comes up to speed, and the inevitable rough patch sometimes causes the hiring manager to prematurely lose faith in the new executive. Referencing gives the hiring manager added confidence that he made the right decision, and that can help him avoid having a rash change of heart while the new hire is still learning.

Second, references give information on how to manage the new executive once he comes on board. References from former bosses are especially helpful because they give a detailed picture of a candidate's accomplishments, working style, and strengths and weaknesses from a manager's perspective. Former managers can also offer advice on how to manage the new hire effectively, and suggest potential problem areas to look out for. A few pearls of wisdom from the candidate's former bosses can help you to ease the candidate's integration into your company and make him (and you) more successful.

## When to Reference

When in the hiring process should you conduct references? Most people don't even ask the question. It is widely assumed that references should be checked after you have narrowed the field to a single finalist. That's the way most companies and most hiring managers do it.

I mostly agree with that approach, but with a significant twist. Whenever possible, I do at least one reference on a candidate before I present him to my client. You could call it a pre-reference.

A pre-reference is qualitatively different from the referencing that happens later in the hiring process. When doing a pre-reference, I'm not digging into the details. In fact, it would be difficult for me to do so because I don't yet know the candidate well enough.

Instead, I'm looking for a very high-level thumbs-up or thumbs-down. Most importantly, I want to know whether the candidate has any fatal flaws. If so, I can avoid wasting time on a candidate who will never work out. It's also helpful to know whether the candidate is a real standout. If that's true, we might decide to put her on a fast track.

I mentally file the responses into three categories. First are the stars. These are the people about whom the reference says something like, "She did an unbelievable job. I loved working with her. She just gets stuff done and doesn't need a lot of handholding. I've tried to hire her since the last time we worked together, but the geography has never worked out. Your client would be lucky to get her."

Second are the solid performers. The reference doesn't show quite as much enthusiasm as he might for a star, but makes it clear the candidate was competent and a good team member.

Last are those who get a bad review. A pre-reference once told me, "I hate to say this because I've never given a bad reference, but he was incredibly divisive. He couldn't get along with anyone on the team and was prone to temper tantrums. I had to fire him. He's a competent guy, and I hate for him to lose out on an opportunity because of my reference, but I have to be honest with you." That reference saved the client and me a lot of time and potential pain.

## The Tiebreaker Reference

Occasionally one of my clients has difficulty choosing between two very strong candidates. In situations like that I often recommend that we conduct references on both candidates as a tiebreaker.

This technique works extremely well, and I've never had a client who remained unable to choose after references were complete.

If you take this route, it's important to be completely transparent with the candidates. If not, each candidate will assume that (pending references) you have decided to extend him an offer. Explain that there are two finalists, and references will help the company make a final decision.

It's not always possible to do a pre-reference. In the majority of cases, I can find someone in my network who has worked with the candidate and will give an unvarnished opinion, but sometimes I can't. Do as much as you can.

Deep referencing comes later, when you've identified a candidate to whom you would likely make an offer. It comes at the end of the process for several reasons.

First, deep referencing is very time-consuming, and it's just not worth doing for every candidate who walks in the door. It would slow the search to a crawl.

Second, it's impossible to do a good job with reference calls until you know the candidate extremely well and have identified specific issues that you would like to explore. It would be a waste of time.

Finally, most candidates (quite understandably) do not want to call on their references until there is a very high probability they will receive an offer. Each reference given on a candidate's behalf represents a favor from a trusted colleague and, as such, requires the candidate to expend some relationship equity. Candidates won't do that unless there's a reasonable probability they will get a job offer in return.

## Building the Reference List

Let's assume you've identified a candidate you would like to hire. You've met him many times and believe you have a good feel for his strengths and weaknesses. You know what issues you would like to explore in references. How many references are enough, and where should the names come from?

Most people, even seasoned HR professionals, don't do nearly enough references. Think about the CEO whose story I told earlier in this chapter. He did three references and thought he had done a good job, but obviously it was inadequate given the unhappy outcome. Three references might be enough if you are evaluating a new house cleaner or lawn service, but it's grossly inadequate when it comes to executive hiring.

So what's the right number? There is no fixed number, but in most cases eight to ten is sufficient. Include all former managers from the last ten years, plus former peers and former subordinates. This yields a comprehensive view of the candidate from all levels of the organization. Keep talking to people until you stop hearing new things and have built a consistent picture of the candidate as a manager, co-worker, and subordinate. When you start hearing the same themes over and over again and there's nothing new, you're done. That won't happen until you've talked with a lot of people.

You should, of course, ask the candidate for a list of references, but don't leave it at that. In addition to candidate-supplied references, I recommend

---

## A Special Situation

Candidates who have worked at the same company for many years can present a considerable challenge when it comes to referencing. For many of them, their most important references are still working at the company, and it's impossible to use them without jeopardizing the candidate's current employment.

For example, I recruited a candidate who had been employed at the same company for eighteen years. He'd had several bosses over that time, and all of them were still employed at the company. The lack of references from immediate supervisors was an obvious and gaping hole in our due diligence, and there wasn't anything we could do about it.

I talked with my client about how he would like to proceed. Fortunately, we had many references from peers and subordinates who had left the company over the years. He was comfortable enough with the references we could get that he felt secure extending an offer, which was accepted.

This is a fairly unusual circumstance, but you'll surely encounter it from time to time. When you do, maximize the references you can get, then decide whether you have enough data to make an informed decision on an offer.

identifying references that are not on the candidate's list. This helps ensure you're getting beyond the candidate's hand-picked choices. Tell candidates you plan to do this and request permission. It's a courtesy, but it also gives them an opportunity to flag people who might be sensitive (for example, a former co-worker who's a close friend of the candidate's current boss). Phrase the question like this: "I'd like to source some references of my own. Is that OK with you? If it is, is there anyone you don't want me to talk to?" In all my years of recruiting no one has ever said no.

Here's a typical referencing scenario. In a recent case, my client and I spoke to eleven references on a candidate. The candidate supplied seven of the names, and I identified the others on my own. My client spoke to several of the most important references himself, and I did the rest. All told I spent about five hours on the phone and another four hours writing up a report summarizing the discussions and my conclusions. The result was a portrait of an outstanding executive. It helped my client feel confident he had made a sound choice, and gave him useful information on how to manage the new executive effectively.

## Preparing for Calls

Once you have a list of references, you are ready to start talking to people. However, before you pick up the phone, take a few minutes to think through your goals.

After multiple interviews with the candidate, it should be easy to identify key issues that you and others would like to explore in depth. Starting from that foundation, build a list of questions.

View these questions as a guide, not a script. Be prepared to take the conversation wherever the reference leads you, because quite often they'll go into unexpected territory. I once spoke to a reference who gave a glowing report on a candidate, then added, "We were all sure he would become CEO until the SEC investigation." It was a surprise and sent the conversation in a completely new direction.

---

### Sample Interview Questions

The questions you ask will be different for every candidate, depending on what issues you wish to explore and what you perceive the candidate's strengths and weaknesses to be. That said, reference calls tend to follow a common structure. Here are a number of sample questions that can serve as a framework for any reference call. The questions have been framed as they would be asked to a former boss, but many of them can be adapted for references with peers and subordinates.

- Establish context: When did you work together, and what was your working relationship?
- What were the candidate's main objectives when you began working together? What did he achieve? Were you happy with the results? What could have been done better?
- How would you describe his personality?
- In what kind of an organization would he do well? Are there situations where he wouldn't be as successful?
- Is he smart?
- Can he accept feedback?
- Did he hire good people? Are they still there?
- Which peers did he need to work with most frequently? How did they get along? Is he a team player?
- Did people like working with and for him?
- How would you rank him against others who have worked for you in the past?
- In what areas did you need to provide the candidate with guidance and help? (This is a less-threatening way to ask about weaknesses and areas where the candidate needed to develop.)
- If he left, why did he leave?
- What advice would you give this person's new boss on managing the candidate?
- Is there anyone else I should talk to who worked with the candidate closely?
- Is there anything you would like to add about the candidate that I haven't asked you about?

As the hiring manager, you should do the most important references yourself. Since doing ten or more references is very time-consuming, it makes sense to get assistance from someone who's expert in referencing, such as a senior-level human resources executive or executive search consultant, to handle the rest of the references. That ensures a thorough job and frees you from many hours of work.

You may be tempted to delegate *all* of the references. Don't do it! Even when you have help from an expert, you must do the key references yourself. I advise my clients to speak to the candidate's two or three most recent managers since they're the ones who can provide the best perspective on strengths and weaknesses as well as advice on how to manage the candidate. If you aren't doing some of the references yourself, you aren't doing your job.

## The Reference Call

I'm often asked whether references can be relied on to provide a realistic view of a candidate. The answer is yes, provided you talk to enough of them and you conduct the calls with some skill. Here are some suggestions.

*Set Expectations.* Most reference calls are cursory affairs in which the person calling for a reference is not really interested in learning anything. As a result, most of the people you call will be looking for signals on how much you want to hear. A simple statement like, "Thanks so much for taking time to talk. This is a critical hire for us, and we take references very seriously," can help to set expectations.

*Dictate the Pace.* You'll be calling very busy people. Don't allow yourself to be rushed—it's important that you determine the pace and do a thorough job. A typical call takes fifteen to thirty minutes, and some take longer. If the reference runs out of time, schedule a follow-up phone call.

*Get Them to Relax.* If you're cold and formal on the phone, no one will want to help you. Be friendly and help the reference to relax. If you're likeable, there's a much greater chance they'll be open. If you share friends or acquaintances, went to the same schools, or have other things in common, take a moment to discuss those points of connection. Then break the ice with simple questions that provide context on the reference's work with the candidate, and move on from there.

*Listen.* Sometimes hiring managers are so enamored with a candidate they overlook subtle red flags. Be open to bad news, or you might not hear it when it's offered. Listen carefully to what's said and unsaid, be prepared for surprises, and follow up when references suggest new lines of questioning.

*Be Persistent.* Some references will give you a frank appraisal without prodding, but others will hold back. Press for real answers. Unwillingness to speak openly about a candidate raises new questions you need to explore.

*Probe.* References tend to couch negative comments in the best possible light. Ask plenty of follow-up questions to be sure you understand what the reference really means. Sometimes a simple comment like, "He's very self-assured," is an oblique way of saying, "He's an egomaniac."

*When Necessary, Be Provocative.* If the description you're hearing is flawless, it may help to show what you already know by bringing up negatives mentioned by other references. For example, "Another reference said a couple of his subordinates didn't like him and wanted to get out of his group. Did you see that?" or "Another reference told me his strategic thinking is weak, and the plan he drafted was flawed. What do you think?" This almost always prompts the reference to be more forthcoming.

*Ask About Unknowns.* You don't know what you don't know. I like to end references calls by asking, "Is there anything I should have asked you about but didn't?" Usually this question is a throwaway, but sometimes it uncovers something new and unexpected. For example, one reference answered, "Yes. Her writing is terrible. It was a problem in our company culture, so I made sure she had an assistant to help edit her written communications."

Most people will respond to your request for a reference quickly, because they want to help the candidate. When they don't, it's a bad sign, usually signaling that they aren't eager to talk. When you get these references on the phone, dig deeply.

Sometimes you'll get someone you know is holding back. No matter how hard you probe, you can't crack him. That happens. Just note that the reference was not helpful and make sure you have enough other references to fill in the blanks.

When you're done referencing, evaluate what you've learned. Document the references in writing, and discuss them with other key players who are involved in the hire. Your colleagues will benefit from what you've learned, and your thorough approach will put to rest any lingering concerns about the candidate and set the stage for his successful entry into the company.

## When the Reference Won't Talk

Very rarely, a reference will refuse to talk with you. The person will either ignore your request, or cite a company policy that prohibits employee references. Occasionally they will refer you to the HR leader, which is just another way to say no.

It doesn't matter what reasons are given for refusing a reference, because it's always a red flag. Yes, it's true that some companies have policies that prohibit their employees from providing references, but these are universally ignored. Supplying and receiving references is an age-old professional courtesy, and executives give them routinely and enthusiastically for outstanding people.

Refusal means the executive has nothing good to say, and also implies that she is worried about the potential legal fallout of telling you the truth. You can safely assume that things ended very badly indeed. Find other references who can provide insight into what happened.

## Common Mistakes

There are three common problems that I see again and again. If you're aware of these before you start the process, you have a far better chance of avoiding them.

First and foremost, many hiring managers make up their minds before they do references. They don't want to learn anything that contradicts their decision. There is no in-depth questioning, no probing for weaknesses and development areas, and an unwillingness to hear bad news. If this is your approach, referencing will be a waste of time.

To be sure, it can be difficult to keep an open mind at this point of the hiring process. There is always pressure to complete an important search as quickly as possible. By the time you get around to references, it's understood that you are almost certain you want to hire the candidate. The key word is *almost*: you must leave the door open, at least a little bit, to changing your mind. If not, why bother with references at all? If you don't engage in a serious process and stay open to information that contradicts your preconceptions, you're certain to miss the subtle comments that lead to the greatest insights.

Second, most hiring managers simply don't talk to enough people. Three or four references are not nearly enough. You have to keep talking to people and pulling on loose ends until you stop hearing new things. That's how you build a complete and nuanced picture of a candidate.

Obviously doing ten or more references is quite time-consuming. That's why I've recommended you enlist an outside recruiter or an internal HR resource for assistance. If you use an internal resource, make sure the person supporting you has enough seniority to be credible. People who are obviously junior won't be taken seriously.

Third, many hiring managers think uncovering negative things is bad. That couldn't be further from the truth. You need to know the strengths and weaknesses of the person you're hiring. Unless your candidate is Jesus, the Buddha, or some other perfect being, the person has flaws. None of us mortals are perfect, and thorough referencing will always highlight weaknesses along with strengths. Not finding any weaknesses is a sure sign you are doing a bad job.

## Summary

References are the single most powerful tool available to hiring managers. If you do them well, references will save you from your own mistakes and dramatically improve your rate of hiring success.

- References help cut through the candidate's self-interested picture of his track record.
- Thorough references will enable you to avoid hiring people who are doomed to fail, and to get more from the people you do end up hiring.
- When possible, do one or two pre-references to get a high-level "good/not good" opinion before you meet candidates.
- Deep references come after you've decided to move toward making an offer to a candidate. Most people do too few references. Eight to ten is usually adequate, but do more if necessary.
- Keep an open mind and do serious, probing references calls.
- Expect to find flaws. If you don't, you're doing a bad job.

## Note

1. Adam Bryant, "Brian Halligan, CEO of HubSpot, on the Value of Naps," Corner Office, *New York Times*, December 5, 2013, http://www.nytimes.com/2013/12/06/business/brian-halligan-chief-of-hubspot-on-the-value-of-naps.html.

# Chapter 8

# Making Offers That Are Accepted

The references went well. You've told the candidate he will receive an offer, and he's excited. It looks like the search will be wrapped up quickly. You relax and say to yourself, "It's as good as done."

Not so fast.

This is the point at which many hiring managers lose focus. That's a mistake, because the search isn't over yet. The deal hasn't been closed, and there is ample time for things to go wrong. It's true, the odds are in your favor, and you're likely to get an acceptance. But you don't have one yet, and you can't allow yourself to relax until you do. Otherwise, you might end up snatching defeat from the jaws of victory.

Creating, presenting, and negotiating a job offer is the final two miles of a marathon. If you maintain concentration and press on with maximum effort, you will complete a successful race. Botch it, and the prior twenty-four miles of effort will be for nothing. Keep running until it's over. There will be plenty of time for celebration after you cross the finish line.

When done well, presentation of the offer is the consummation of an extremely positive courtship. It generates significant goodwill and leaves the candidate with enthusiasm for his new job and eagerness to get started. He begins work with an attitude that creates optimal conditions for his success—and yours.

With so much at stake in getting it right, it's surprising that a significant percentage of hiring managers and their companies do a poor job making offers. Viewed from a high level, there are two ways things go wrong.

One is by making an offer that is unattractive, because the candidate has been left with unrealistic expectations, no one asked what's important to her, or the company is trying to get a bargain. When the offer is too far off the mark, the candidate feels disappointment that quickly turns into frustration and anger. Discussions start in a bad place, and sometimes it's difficult to recover.

The second common mistake is presenting the offer in a thoughtless, impersonal way, like a marriage proposal sent via text message. Just as a marriage proposal requires a personal touch, so does presentation of an offer.

The manner in which the offer is presented is important because we are dealing with human beings. For all but the most mercenary people, work is about much more than money. Everyone wants to be compensated fairly, but they also care deeply about having stimulating work, talented colleagues, and an environment where they are appreciated and valued.

When a hiring manager has no involvement in making the offer, he sends the message that the candidate is not a high priority. That leaves the candidate feeling that the company views hiring her as just another of countless business transactions. That can be deeply unsettling. She says to herself, "I'm not feeling great about this now, and I don't even work there yet. What's it going to be like if I join? It's certainly not likely to get better."

The worst outcome is when mismanagement of the offer leads to rejection. That sends the search back to the beginning, which means higher recruiting expenses, an important job going unfilled, and the potential for damage to the hiring manager's reputation within the company.

Even when a bungled offer is accepted, it exacts a toll. It causes the candidate to begin his new job with misgivings and doubt instead of enthusiasm. That doesn't create a strong foundation for success.

This chapter will teach you how to make offers that will be accepted. It covers constructing the offer, presenting it in the most appealing way possible, managing negotiations, and what to do after receiving an acceptance. In addition, there are sections on common signs of trouble, and how to recover after an offer is rejected.

All of the topics discussed in this chapter are governed by the recruiting version of the Golden Rule: Treat the candidate the way you'd like to be treated if you were in his position. You should expect him to treat you with the same courtesy, too. Trouble starts when either party strays from that path. When that happens, it can quickly lead to bruised egos, hot emotions, erosion of trust, and negotiations that end in failure.

Let's begin with construction of the offer.

## Constructing the Offer

In your first meeting, you (or your recruiting partner) and the candidate discussed his current compensation plan and the target compensation range for the position. You also covered items like stock options and deferred compensation that might make it expensive for the candidate to leave his job. As a result of those discussions, you've minimized the possibility of unpleasant surprises. Both sides should have reasonable expectations, and see potential to come to an agreement that's fair and equitable to both parties.

Now you must figure out the details of a job offer. Where do you begin? Let's start with the items that are most commonly included in an offer letter.

## Elements of the Offer

What's in the offer varies considerably depending on the size of the company and its internal norms. At a minimum, the offer defines base salary and notes eligibility for benefits like insurance and retirement plans. Most offers have a good deal more than that, including bonus compensation and long-term incentives. Here are some of the items that might be found in the offer letter:

- *Base salary.*
- *Bonus* (usually expressed as a percentage of base salary). This is discretionary compensation that is tied to achievement of some combination of personal, corporate, and sometimes departmental or divisional objectives.
- *Long-term incentives.* These can include stock options, restricted stock grants, or other similar items. Regardless of the form, long-term incentives usually vest over several years. They are powerful retention tools because they can make it expensive for a valued employee to leave the company.
- *Severance.* Usually reserved for very senior executives.
- *Relocation assistance.* For candidates who must relocate. Terms vary greatly depending on a company's size and resources.
- *Insurance coverage.*
- *Retirement plans.*
- *Car allowance.*
- *Sign-on bonus.* Sometimes offered to help offset loss of long-term compensation. Sign-on bonuses can also be used to sweeten an offer with a one-time payment instead of increasing base salary and bonus.

Partner with your human resources group on creation of the offer. A good HR executive will help you figure out how to make an offer that's fair and attractive, and is compliant with the company's policies.

If you don't have an HR group—for example, if you're an entrepreneur or small business owner with a small staff—you may find it helpful to consult with a trusted colleague or an HR consultant when constructing the offer. The issues are fairly simple, but if you make major mistakes, it can be expensive to correct them.

You should also have the offer reviewed by a lawyer who has extensive experience with employment agreements. Guide the legal review with a firm hand: you want the finished product to have the feel of a verbal handshake, not a cold and impersonal legal document. If you don't provide guidance, the lawyer may seek to protect you against every possible contingency, and if that happens, the offer letter will end up resembling a nuclear arms treaty.

## Find Out What's Important to the Candidate

If you ask the candidate about her priorities, you may learn something important that enables you to craft an offer that's especially enticing. Don't assume you know what she values, or that her priorities are the same as yours. They may not be.

If you want to know what's important to the candidate, ask. If you do, you're more likely to start with an offer that makes the candidate feel good and leads to a successful conclusion.

Quite often you will learn there is a critical factor that has nothing to do with money. Here's an example. I recruited an outstanding executive to run marketing for one of my clients. She was one of the best at her function I'd ever met, but I almost passed on her because her compensation was so far below the norm. I assumed she couldn't possibly be senior enough for the job I was trying to fill. Fortunately I kept an open mind long enough to realize she was a gem.

Why was her compensation so low? She had two young children, and flexible working hours were important to her. Although she was being paid only 60 percent of her market value, her employer was located near her house and gave her great latitude with her schedule. That enabled her to be home to get her children on the school bus in the morning and to pick them up in the late afternoon. At that time in her life, the ability to define her own schedule was worth more than money. It must be noted that flexible hours did not mean less work. In fact, she had an intense work ethic and worked many more hours than her peers.

My client offered her a substantial raise, but that wasn't the decisive factor. She wouldn't have accepted if the company had not made it clear that she could continue to define her own schedule. She took the job and has been a star.

Ask the candidate what's really important to her. Get past mere money to the things that matter to her personal life. If you can address these in the offer, you're almost sure to get an acceptance, along with an employee who's committed and loyal.

## Put Together the Numbers

Sit down with your recruiting or HR partner to define the numbers. You will need all of the relevant facts, including the candidate's current compensation, market data for similar positions, and the realities of the company's internal compensation structure.

Now it's time to show the candidate you are true to your word. I counsel my clients to lead with an offer they believe is fair and equitable. Of course, that doesn't mean you need to give the candidate everything he wants. The offer should be fair to both sides and leave room for minor adjustments through negotiation.

Don't lowball the offer. The objective should not be to hire the candidate for the lowest possible price. Rather, you're seeking to negotiate a deal that works for your company, compensates the new executive appropriately given the market, and gives him the right incentives. A good offer leaves both sides feeling they have a fair deal, and leaves you room to increase the executive's compensation over time.

Don't go too high, either. Know what you're comfortable paying and what makes business sense, and stick to your guns. Candidates who want to join for the right reasons will respond positively to a fair deal. Mercenaries who fight to squeeze every nickel from an offer generally don't perform well once they're on the job.

Sometimes it can be tricky to navigate issues of internal equity. Whatever the internal norms, your offer must make sense for the candidate and should reflect the market for the job. You need to create an offer the candidate will find attractive, without venturing so far outside of company precedent that you set up the new hire for failure. If your company's salary structure cannot accommodate the candidate's needs, you've already committed a critical error and should be looking at less pricey candidates.

### We Don't Have to Pay Market

Most of us see our employers through rose-colored glasses, and this is especially true for entrepreneurs. Sometimes this enthusiasm translates into an expectation that a candidate will accept a sub-par offer because he wants to work with you so badly. In very rare instances that may be true, but most of the time it is wishful thinking. The best candidates expect and can demand exciting work and competitive compensation. There are many other exciting companies that pay the market rate for talent, so don't expect a bargain.

# MAKING THE OFFER

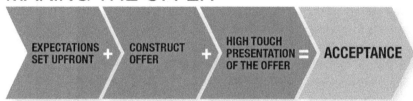

I encourage my clients to put a deadline on job offers. Over the course of the interview process, the candidate has ample time for due diligence and discussions with his family, so if it takes forever to make a decision once the offer arrives, something is wrong.

A deadline sets expectations and serves notice to the candidate that he can't take forever to get back to you with an answer. A week is usually more than enough time, and it should never take more than two weeks. It's important to note that deadlines are mostly symbolic and are almost never strictly observed, as long as progress is being made toward an agreement.

Finally, don't expect your initial offer to be the last word. There is almost always some back and forth, so expect negotiation. If the initial offer is reasonable, issues are usually easy to resolve.

## Presenting the Offer

Once the offer has been put in writing, you're ready to present it to the candidate. How you present it will have a major impact on how it's received. Don't text the marriage proposal! Even if the offer is compelling, you must present it in a way that communicates how much you want the candidate to join your team, and that restates all of the reasons he should say yes. That requires your personal involvement.

The best candidates have multiple job opportunities. Why does a candidate select one job over another? Sometimes it's money, but more often it's intangibles that have to do with human relationships. All other things being equal, the deciding factor is how the candidates *feels* about the people with whom he'll be working—and especially you, his potential boss. That's why the personal touch is so important. If the candidate doesn't feel a connection with you and members of your team, he'll go to work for someone else.

When you believe the offer will be readily accepted, and if geography and schedules allow, presenting it to the candidate in person is the best option. One of my clients, Fred, is the president of a large technology company. He handles presentation of offers with unusual skill, and his method is a useful case study.

Fred invites the candidate to his office for a meeting at which he presents the offer letter. It's a relaxed and cordial one-on-one, and there are no HR people involved. He spends an hour or so walking the candidate through each feature of the offer.

During the meeting, he also explains the thinking behind the offer by putting it into the context of the company's broader compensation philosophy. He says something like, "We aren't the highest-paying company. We pay somewhere near the median for our industry. But you will make a lot of money here if you do well. We believe in paying for performance, and the offer includes incentives that have the potential to reward you handsomely if you contribute to the team's success." He backs that up with examples from the current executive team, all of whom have done quite well.

Finally—and this is really important—he uses the meeting to move toward closing the deal. He restates why he believes the candidate is a great fit for the job and the company culture, and tells the candidate he's excited by the prospect of having him join the team. It's a powerful message, not least because it's absolutely genuine and sincere.

Fred's approach is the best, but what if distance or travel schedules make it difficult or impossible to meet in person? If that's the case, cover the same ground in a phone call. Try to schedule it for a time when neither side will be rushed (evenings or weekends often work well for these discussions). A phone call isn't nearly as good as meeting in person, but it's the next best thing if a face-to-face meeting can't happen, or can't happen quickly.

Presenting the offer yourself is best if you expect things to go smoothly, but what if you anticipate a difficult negotiation? If you're not sure how the offer will be received, consider having a third party—like your recruiter or HR partner—present it on your behalf. This enables you to avoid the potential for an uncomfortable situation. If the offer lands with a thud, emotions on both sides can escalate rapidly. Having a buffer between you and the candidate can keep things cool when negotiations get difficult.

Having a third party present the offer doesn't absolve you from the need to be involved. Only you can provide the personal outreach that will make the candidate feel good about accepting the job.

Do what feels right and authentic to you. When you've determined that you'll be extending an offer, call the candidate to let her know. Say something like, "You'll be hearing from someone on my team with a formal job offer. I am very excited about the possibility of you joining us. We can achieve great things together. I know you'll make an important contribution, and we'll enjoy working together. The whole team is really excited. I'm looking forward to getting you on board."

## Negotiating

Don't expect the initial offer to be accepted immediately. Sometimes that happens, but it's rare. It's much more common for there to be issues— sometimes minor and sometimes more consequential—that must be worked through before you come to an agreement.

Candidates know they will never have more leverage than they do at the moment they've received an offer, so you shouldn't be surprised when they try to negotiate the most favorable deal possible. However, the way the candidate handles these discussions will tell you a lot about your odds of success.

When a candidate responds with a positive attitude and in a spirit of collaboration, things are almost certain to work out. She might say something like, "Thank you for the offer. I am really excited about this opportunity and the prospect of joining the company and working with you. I want this job. There are a few issues that I'd like to discuss with you, to see if there's a way we can adjust them. Let me explain what they are and why they are important to me."

Of course, you must approach negotiations with the same positive attitude and be open to the possibility of modifying the terms of the offer. If your initial offer was attractive and reasonable, it will be easy to work out the details.

What do I mean by details? The most common requests are for modifications to cash compensation (usually the base), the stock option grant, vacation time, and severance.

If you've left yourself some latitude on base salary and you think the candidate's request is reasonable, consider your options. There will be times when you decide to make a modest adjustment to show the candidate you are listening and willing to compromise. That doesn't mean you need to match what the candidate has requested. Make a judgment based on the unique circumstances of the situation.

At other times, you may decide to push back. After all, if you're talking about small stuff in the context of the entire offer, it's unlikely to tip things one way or another. You might respond by saying something like, "I'm not going to adjust the salary. I think we've put together offer that's fair, and it's a great opportunity for you. You have to look at the offer in its entirety. I can't imagine that a relatively modest adjustment would make the difference between this being the right or wrong fit. I think you know that in the long run you'll do extremely well here if you perform."

If you decide to make a change, increases should be modest, by which I mean no more than 10 percent. If you and the candidate are discussing larger changes, that's a symptom of another problem. Perhaps your initial offer was far too low. If so, you may need to bite the bullet and increase cash compensation to a more appropriate level. It's also possible that the candidate's request is simply unreasonable. If so, be prepared to explain why it doesn't make sense.

Requests for a larger stock option grant are especially common at venture-backed companies. In fact, many startup veterans focus more on the option grant than cash compensation because they see options, quite rightly, as their path to build wealth. If your company is a startup and the candidate wants more options, take it as a positive sign that demonstrates the candidate has the right mindset.

Discussions about stock options have a tendency to become ungrounded, especially if the candidate is not a seasoned startup veteran. Fortunately, there's extensive data on the size of initial stock option grants for different functions and at different stages in a company's development. Use the data to keep the discussion anchored in facts. As long as you are willing to make a market-level option grant, and the candidate expects no more than that, you'll reach an agreement quickly.

What about severance agreements? I know of many large companies that do not offer severance agreements to anyone, as a matter of policy. On the other end of the spectrum, there are high-risk companies (like turn-arounds) where the probability of business failure is so high that no one will join unless severance is part of the deal. At most companies, however, severance agreements are offered to only a small group of the most senior executives.

Your company's policy on severance will dictate your approach. If your company doesn't have a policy on granting severance to executives, think long and hard before you agree to give it to anyone. It could become an expensive precedent.

What about vacation? Talking about vacation can seem trivial, but it almost always comes up. Company policies on vacation vary widely, and it isn't unusual for a candidate to be faced with a big drop in vacation time when joining a new employer.

I've never seen the issue of vacation time get in the way of making a deal. If your company will allow you to match the candidate's current vacation time, do it.

However, sometimes it's not that simple. Many companies won't make exceptions to their vacation policies, because they don't want to set a precedent that could be perceived to be unfair—or that could snowball into a wholesale erosion of vacation policies, with important financial implications.

If that's your situation, there's a simple solution. Many clients will make a handshake agreement, saying, "Look, I'm not at liberty to deviate from the vacation policy. I don't want to set the wrong precedent by doing that. But I understand why you want more vacation time, and I don't have a problem with you taking more time off as long as you're getting your work done." Working it out this way requires trust on both sides.

One final point: don't make concessions you'll regret later. Negotiating can be stressful, especially when you are under pressure to get a new executive on board. When you stand your ground, you open yourself to the possibility that the deal will fall through, and that can be intensely uncomfortable. Sometimes it's tempting to give in just to get the search finished.

If you're feeling that temptation, resist it. It's one thing to make a reasonable compromise, but quite another to agree to something that you don't believe makes sense or that will undermine you in the long term. Caving in and making a bad deal sets everyone up for failure.

## Bad Karma: Signs of Trouble

When the candidate is motivated to join and you've made a reasonable offer, discussions tend to go smoothly and amicably. There's a spirit of "Let's make this work."

Sometimes, however, things go wrong. The friendly discussion you'd hoped for doesn't materialize, and things get rocky. How can you tell if a deal is headed south? Here are some red flags that indicate you're headed for trouble.

## The Candidate Wants Excessive Time

By the time you make an offer, the candidate has had abundant time to learn about the job, the company, and you. He knows—or should know—whether he wants the job. It's reasonable for the candidate to take time to confirm that his family is on board, do a final analysis of the company, and understand the details of your offer, but those tasks shouldn't take more than a few days.

Given those considerations, how long should it take for a candidate to make a decision about a job offer? How long is too long? In my opinion, it shouldn't take more than a week to get a response. If it does (barring extenuating circumstances), it's a sign that the candidate may not be as interested as you thought.

If the candidate asks for an extension or gives you some other reason to think he is delaying a decision, it's time to address the matter directly. I'll say something like, "It's taking you a long time to make a decision. You seem to be ambivalent about this opportunity. What's going on? The client is starting to think you're not interested." That usually provokes a response that sheds light on the situation.

There are plenty of benign reasons a candidate might want more time. Perhaps the candidate's spouse is traveling and she hasn't been able to discuss the job offer with him in person. Maybe a family member needs to be convinced to accept the move. If there's a genuine need for more time, then grant it.

Most of the likely reasons for delay are more problematic. Perhaps the candidate is waiting for a competing offer, or is using your offer as a lever to get more from his current employer. Maybe his spouse or children are revolting against the idea of relocation now that it's become a concrete possibility. Perhaps he is simply getting cold feet about changing jobs, in which case you may justifiably wonder whether he can make tough decisions.

If you conclude that the candidate isn't really interested, be prepared to withdraw the offer. It can be difficult to accept that things won't work out, but there's no point in denying reality or delaying the inevitable.

If you have a strong number-two candidate waiting in the wings, you have an especially powerful incentive to withdraw the offer. After all, it would be doubly painful to lose your backup candidate because you let things drag out with your first choice. When it becomes clear that things won't work out, move on.

### The Candidate Makes Unreasonable Demands

Rarely, a candidate will respond to an offer with compensation demands that are far above the range you discussed earlier in the process, or that simply don't make sense given her salary history. What the candidate is telling you is that she isn't seriously interested unless you provide a windfall.

Candidates who do this are mercenaries. They don't care about the company, the team, or the mission. They're only interested in selling their services to the highest bidder. Negotiating with such a candidate can feel like talking with a used car dealer.

This isn't the way most executives operate. Money is important to everyone, of course, but for most people it's one of many factors to be considered when looking at a new job. They want to be paid fairly, but they also want to do interesting and challenging work with like-minded and talented colleagues. In short, they want work that is enjoyable and fulfilling.

If you are unlucky enough to hire a mercenary, you'll end up with a radically self-centered executive who will poison your company and destroy your team. The only silver lining is that the executive won't stay for long. He'll move on as soon as there's a better offer.

I've never seen a situation where a candidate's unreasonable demands resulted in him getting hired. There's simply no way to salvage this situation, and you should not want to do so. Cut your losses as quickly as possible and move on to other candidates who are interested in the job for the right reasons.

In every case, mercenaries could have been identified and screened out long before you got to the point of making an offer. But if you find yourself in this situation, there's no point in beating yourself up. Try to learn from the experience so you don't face the same thing in the future.

## Acceptance and Finishing

When things go well, negotiations end with the candidate's acceptance. Acceptance is always a cause for celebration, and the hiring manager, HR, and the recruiter can congratulate one another on a job well done. The hiring manager feels a great sense of relief that the long process has ended successfully.

But it's still not over—at least, not quite yet. The search isn't really done until the new executive is sitting at her desk.

Acceptance of the offer marks the beginning of a period of limbo that lasts until the candidate's start date. It's a risky time when there's still ample opportunity for things to go wrong. In other words, it's no time to relax.

In this period between acceptance and start date, it's important to continue regular communication with the candidate. Doing so demonstrates how excited you are to have the new executive join the company. Without it, the contrast between the way you courted the candidate during negotiations and the silence after his acceptance will be jarring and unsettling.

Second, you have an opportunity to begin engaging the new executive immediately after his acceptance, even though he hasn't formally started. The period between jobs is a great time for the new executive to begin learning everything he will need to know as he comes up to speed. Give the new executive as much material as he can absorb. As he dives into it, he will mentally make the transition to his new job, even if he isn't physically there yet.

Finally, it's important to stay in touch, to make sure your company is following through by providing the information and assistance promised during negotiations. If the executive is relocating, for example, make sure your company is meeting its commitments and making the process as painless as possible. See whether there are other ways you or the company can help to make the transition easier for the candidate and his family.

### Major Risks

After you've received an acceptance, there's still a possibility the deal could fall apart. I've seen this happen in two ways.

The first is related to relocation. Earlier in this book, I told the story of a candidate I recruited to run marketing at a very high-growth technology company. He planned to relocate with his family from California to New England. Then, three days before his start date, his wife announced she wasn't going to move. That scuttled the deal.

I don't think there's anything we could have done to change that outcome. It was driven by family and marital dynamics that we could not see or change. We had done everything we could think of to introduce the candidate and his wife to the region and to make their transition easy.

This story highlights the major risk associated with relocation. You're often moving a family, not just one person, and there are a host of risks that you may never see. The best way to mitigate them is to make sure the candidate has everything she needs to keep her family happy. Make sure her spouse has plenty of time to explore the area, preferably with someone who can show it off in the best possible light. If the spouse needs to find new employment, do everything you can to assist with that process. If there are children and a need to identify a new school, see if you can to help. Try to

---

### Don't Forget the Background Check

Make sure the candidate agrees to a background check as part of his acceptance of the offer.

It's tempting to skip this step, particularly in smaller companies where it's not done as a matter of course. In the vast majority of cases, the background check is purely a formality and doesn't turn up anything. Very rarely it will reveal a frightening skeleton in the candidate's closet, and if that happens you'll be thankful.

Back in 2004, Smith and Wesson announced that their chairman had resigned after the company discovered he had spent time in prison for a string of armed robberies.[1] I'm sure they wish they had conducted a background check.

---

create conditions for the new executive's family to have a successful transition and integration into their new home. If her family is miserable, the candidate won't perform at her best and may end up leaving.

The other way I've seen deals fall apart is when the candidate rescinds his acceptance after receiving a counteroffer. It's exceptionally rare for this to happen at the executive level, because candidates know it burns bridges with both the new company and the old one.

Accepting a counteroffer—or worse, trying to use one as a bargaining chip—signals a lack of integrity and an inability to make a decision that sticks. If you lose a candidate to a counteroffer, it's someone you're better off not hiring anyway.

## Recovering from Rejection

In the vast majority of cases—in my experience, more than 90 percent of the time—the story has a happy ending, and the offer is accepted. But what about those instances when it's not?

If you hire enough people, a rejected offer is something you will face sooner or later. It's always an unwelcome change of plan that requires a scramble to regroup. In the immediate aftermath of a rejection, you may find yourself tempted to blame yourself or point fingers at others. This is always counterproductive. Take time to figure out what went wrong, but don't dwell on any mistakes. Learn from them and move on.

It may be comforting to know that, often, a rejected offer is an unexpected gift, although it never feels like one at the time. If the candidate says no, often it's a sign of some subtle (or not so subtle) incompatibility that would have become a problem. In these cases, the short-term pain of a rejection is nothing compared to the pain you might have endured if the candidate had accepted. With time, you may consider yourself lucky that things didn't work out.

What's the best way to recover from a rejected offer? If the job is vacant, begin by figuring out how you will get the work done until the new executive can be brought on board. That probably means a continuation of whatever interim strategy you've employed since the search began.

You must also reset expectations within the organization. Make sure everyone knows that the timeline for hiring the new executive has been pushed out. Ask for their continued commitment and support until the search is completed.

Once you've regrouped, decide whether you have a viable backup candidate. If you do, you may have an opportunity to salvage the situation with minimal lost time. Reengage with this second candidate as quickly as possible.

Sometimes, reengaging with the backup candidate is delicate. If he knows you made an offer to someone else, he will probably ask you what happened. He may be wondering whether the other candidate found some flaw in the job that he didn't observe. Be prepared to answer his questions and to put the best spin possible on the rejection.

If the candidate knows he was the second choice, he may also wonder whether you really want him. He may say to himself, "Two weeks ago I was a reject, and now they want to hire me. How much do they really want me on board? Will I always be viewed as the second choice? Does that put me in a weak position the moment I walk in the door?" You must make a concerted effort to reassure his bruised ego and make him feel valued and wanted.

What if there is no backup? If that's really true, then there's nothing to do but develop more candidates. But before concluding that no one you've met is viable, I would urge you to re-examine the other candidates with an open mind.

Over the years, I've observed that very few hiring managers will hire the backup candidate (if there was one). Quite often, this has more to do with psychological factors then the candidate's capabilities.

Here's what I mean. Deciding between two highly qualified candidates is usually difficult, because very little separates them. Each has a unique set of strengths and weaknesses, but both are supremely capable. Choosing one over the other is an exercise in interpreting shades of gray.

Yet as the hiring manager approaches a decision, nuances are thrown out the window. He ends up exaggerating the positive qualities of one candidate and emphasizing the negatives of the other. Shades of gray become black and white. The lead candidate's positive qualities are exaggerated, and the negatives are downplayed. The opposite happens with the other candidate, who suddenly becomes undesirable.

That's why it makes sense to think hard about whether the number-two candidate should remain on the scrap heap. What was it that attracted you to that candidate in the first place? Are the negatives as bad as you imagine? Review the candidate's qualifications carefully. It's quite possible you have a highly qualified person right under your nose. If so, you have an opportunity to get back on track quickly.

If none of the other candidates are good enough, then it's time to get back to work developing more. In some respects this is like starting over, and it will take several months to find someone new. Make sure your HR partner and recruiter are committed to going back into the trenches, and then get to work.

## Summary

There's a natural tendency to relax when you're at the point of making an offer. Don't do it! This is the point at which you must focus especially hard on bringing the search to a successful conclusion.

- Before constructing the offer, ask the candidate what's important to her.
- Draft the offer in the spirit of proposing a deal that is fair and equitable to both sides.
- Present the offer with a personal touch. If possible, do it in person.
- Be prepared to negotiate. Make smart compromises, but don't make any concessions you will regret later.
- Look out for common signs of trouble. If you conclude that negotiations are doomed to fail, withdraw the offer and move on.
- If the candidate accepts, it's still not over. Stay in contact until he starts work.
- If the offer is rejected, look again at the other candidates to determine whether you have a backup. If so, reengage her without delay. If not, get back to work developing additional candidates.

## Note

1. Vanessa O'Connell, "How Troubled Past Finally Caught Up With James Minder," *Wall Street Journal*, March 8, 2004, http://online.wsj.com/news/articles/ SB107870298403448693

# Chapter 9

# You Thought You Were Done? After the Hire

One day, some weeks after accepting the job offer, the new executive will take a seat at her desk and begin work. This start date marks the formal end of the search. Completion of the search is a cause for celebration, and it's worth taking a moment to appreciate the accomplishment.

At this point, many hiring managers turn their attention to other matters. The desire to do so is understandable. In all likelihood, important tasks and initiatives have received less attention than deserved while the hiring manager was occupied recruiting a new executive. Now, those things require renewed focus. The hiring manager moves on.

The new executive is left to fend for herself. There's much to learn and very little time to do it. She must rapidly become expert in the business, the players, the dynamics of the company's culture, and the problems and opportunities facing her group. It will take months before she is integrated into the company and can begin to make a meaningful contribution.

Meanwhile, it's not long before the hiring manager and the new executive's peers stop viewing her as the new kid on the block. In their eyes, she rapidly transforms from a new arrival into a full-fledged team member, and that means they expect results. In short order, they begin to form opinions about her competence and effectiveness.

This is the challenge faced by every new executive. Opinions about his performance begin to harden well before he masters the job. Success requires rapid learning and, simultaneously, having an immediate impact. It's like learning to ride a bicycle while competing in the Tour de France.

In his outstanding book *The First 90 Days*, Michael Watkins proposes that new leaders have only ninety days to prove their value in a new position. The new leader must rapidly win the trust and respect of her boss, her peers, and her team. If not, it's impossible to be effective.[1]

The executive who doesn't win trust early will pay the price. At worst he'll be terminated, and at best he'll find his influence greatly diminished. In either case, his career trajectory goes from vertical to horizontal.

This is the fate of far too many new executives. Statistics indicate that a shocking proportion of new hires fail. Joseph Daniel McCool, an authority on executive search and the author of *Deciding Who Leads*, cites one study which found that as many as 40 percent of new executives who were hired from outside failed within eighteen months.[2]

The cost of this astounding failure rate is astronomical. In his bestseller *Topgrading*, Brad Smart estimates the cost of a failed executive hire to be 14.6 times base salary.[3] I don't believe it's possible to calculate the costs so precisely, but his point is indisputable. You don't need a calculator to understand that the financial stakes of a failed hire—including things like recruiting fees, management time, severance, and most importantly, opportunity cost—are very high.

Some executives don't make it because selecting them in the first place was a mistake; they simply aren't well suited to the jobs for which they were recruited. Indeed, this book so far has focused on mastering the selection of new executives so that those mistakes are minimized or eliminated.

Yet not all executives fail because they were poor selections. Sometimes very talented individuals don't make it because something went wrong in the early days of their employment. For whatever reason, they get off on the wrong foot. When an otherwise capable executive fails in this manner, it's like a healthy child, full of potential, who's struck down by a preventable disease. It doesn't have to happen.

The sobering statistics beg the question of whether anything can be done to improve the stick rate of new hires. The answer is a resounding yes, and that's the subject of the rest of this chapter.

## Can You Help New Executives Succeed?

Is it possible that you could take steps to support and accelerate integration of a new executive into the company? Would that raise the odds he would succeed?

The answer to both questions is yes. There are things you can do to accelerate integration, and these steps will help new executives be successful. More executives will succeed, more will achieve their full potential, and they will become productive more quickly than if left on their own.

In the human resources world, the process of helping a new employee make a successful transition into a new job is called *onboarding*. In the context of an executive hire, onboarding means devising a plan to help the new executive rapidly understand the business, its problems, personalities, and politics. It also means helping him garner quick victories that win the confidence of the people around him and help establish his authority in the new position.

At this point I suspect some readers are deeply skeptical. Perhaps you are one of them. You may be saying to yourself, "Onboarding sounds like HR-speak, and HR is out of touch." Indeed, some of my clients, especially CEOs of small and medium-size companies, reflexively think any idea that originates in human resources is a waste of time and money. I don't share that opinion, but if that's your outlook, try to maintain an open mind for just a moment. If you think the word *onboarding* smacks of jargon, feel free to call it something more down-to-earth, like *bringing new executives up to speed*.

In my own work, I avoid the word *onboarding* with clients because it elicits a reflexive, negative reaction from so many people. Instead, I'll talk with them about the actions that must be taken to make a new executive productive. For the sake of clarity and simplicity, however, we'll continue to use the word *onboarding* in this chapter.

If you put your prejudices aside, you'll discover that onboarding is a powerful tool. The fact is, helping new executives find their footing quickly will save many from failure and improve their performance. That means you will enjoy more success, too.

Here's an anecdote from outside the business world, to illustrate the value of onboarding. When my son was ten years old, we moved to a new town. He was a hockey player and joined a local team. It was a tight group, and most of the boys on the team had played together for years.

My son got off to a slow start. On the ice, he was tentative and played without confidence. In the locker room he was quiet, the opposite of his usually exuberant self. He was learning a new system and building relationships with his teammates all at the same time, and it was obvious he found it overwhelming.

Then one day he suddenly received a flurry of invitations from other boys on the team to play after school, attend birthday parties, and things like that. He happily accepted and began to make some friends. As he began feeling more integrated into the group, his play improved.

I realized later that the coach had orchestrated those invitations. He knew hockey inside out, but he knew ten-year-old boys even better. He needed my son to be productive, and realized that helping him to integrate faster would improve his game and help him make a bigger contribution to the team. It worked.

Most coaches wouldn't have made that effort. They would let a new kid sink or swim on his own. My son's coach was proactive in helping him along, because he had great ambitions for his team and needed every player to contribute to the best of his ability. The approach was incredibly effective.

## Old School: Throw 'Em in the Deep End

Onboarding of new executives is still the exception rather than the rule. Most companies follow the time-honored "sink or swim" approach, and throw new hires into the deep end of the pool to see if they drown. That means they leave it to the new executive to figure out what he needs to learn, what relationships need to be built, where the minefields are, what constitutes success, and how to go about achieving it.

There's a kernel of wisdom in the old-style approach. It is entirely reasonable to expect a new executive to take responsibility for his own success. After all, these are very senior people who are highly compensated; shouldn't they be able to make a go of it without handholding? Can't a new executive educate himself, forge the right relationships, set appropriate expectations, and then deliver results?

The short answer to those questions is yes. You have every right to expect a new executive to make his own way. Most companies take this approach, and many executives do fine at managing these transitions when left on their own.

The long answer, however, is more nuanced. Although it may be reasonable to expect a new executive to handle the transition alone, it doesn't always work. A significant percentage of new hires will fail to navigate the transition successfully. When thrown into the deep end, they sink. Sometimes it is their fault, but other times they are ground up by an especially unwelcoming or byzantine corporate culture that would be difficult for anyone to navigate. Whatever the reason, their failure to adapt to a new environment, or to do it fast enough, comes at great cost to their employers and to their own careers.

There's considerable data showing that retention of new hires improves when the company takes a proactive role in onboarding. McCool cites the example of Bristol-Myers Squibb, which increased retention of new executives from 40 to 90 percent by revamping their hiring process, including instituting a formal process for new executive integration.[4]

Business people love data, and the data suggests that onboarding pays a very handsome return. Yet most companies don't do onboarding in any kind of consistent or systematic way. The resistance to onboarding is undeniable. Why is this case, when there are such compelling reasons to do it? Let's look at a few of the reasons.

The first is purely cultural. There's a lingering perception, left over from the Dark Ages of management thinking, that any senior executive who needs or accepts help is a weakling. This is not uncommon in companies with scrappy, tough-guy cultures. Those who view the world this way see onboarding as a form of remedial education rather than as a tool that unlocks the best possible executive performance.

The second reason is financial. Even though it's intuitively obvious that onboarding saves money, sometimes it doesn't look that way to the finance people. Although the results of a comprehensive initiative such as the one at Bristol-Myers Squibb can be quantified, the results of any individual onboarding project are impossible to measure. Short of cloning the executive and running a controlled experiment, there's no way to prove that she profited from the experience. That makes it easy to tag onboarding as yet another HR program that adds cost but doesn't deliver measureable results.

If you're from the old school, you have a decision to make. Sure, you can take an ideological approach and reject onboarding on principle. You can pound your fist on the desk and say, "I'm not holding anybody's hand. Let him figure it out on his own." If you do, however, know that your decision isn't supported by data or common sense. Leaving new executives to fend for themselves will be costly for them, for your company, and ultimately for you and your career.

## What Needs to Be Done?

I'm going to assume you are at least open to the possibility that onboarding can be valuable. Let's review what needs to be done. What exactly does a new executive need to learn, and what action does she need to take, in order to become effective?

Viewed from a very high level, the work of onboarding falls into two categories. The first is learning, which includes learning about the business, the executive's functional area, the people in the company with whom the new executive will work, and the company culture.

The second category is setting expectations. Working together with you, the new executive needs to identify the problems and opportunities in his functional area, and then establish short-term and long-term objectives.

# THINGS TO LEARN

| THE BUSINESS | THE DEPARTMENT | PEOPLE | POLITICS | CULTURE |
| --- | --- | --- | --- | --- |

The short-term objectives are particularly important because they enable the new executive to rapidly establish his value, credibility, and leadership.

The volume of things to absorb is daunting. Consider the syllabus for the executive's crash course in his new job. It includes learning the business, department, people, politics, and culture. It would be nice to tackle those subjects one at a time, but the new executive doesn't have that luxury. Instead, everything hits at once in a dizzying fusillade. It can be overwhelming.

Let's take a quick look at each of those areas, and then touch on the subject of setting expectations.

### The Business

Before she walks in the door, the new executive has done her homework. She's studied the numbers, the products, the documents you provided in advance, and anything else she could get her hands on. In short, she'll start with an excellent high-altitude view of the business.

Yet it's not nearly enough. Of course, understanding the business from a high level is essential, but it won't help the new executive accomplish anything. There's a big difference between theory (understanding the business at a high level) and practice (knowing how to get things done). All the strategic insight in the world won't help a new executive who can't pull the appropriate levers and push the right buttons to make things happen.

Learning all of the intricacies of a new business will take a year or more. In the early days, a new executive doesn't need to know everything, but he does need to learn fast enough to begin making decisions, taking action, and avoiding stupid mistakes.

### The Department

In addition to learning about the dynamics of the business, the new executive, if he is a functional leader, must master what's going on in his own functional area. What's going well? Where are opportunities for improvement? Is there agreement on the key problems? If changes are needed, when and how they should be implemented?

Most important of all, the new executive must assess his team and determine whether he has the right people to accomplish the mission. If not, he needs to figure out how to make changes while minimizing disruption.

## People

We just touched on the people in the new executive's team. However, there are a host of other important relationships to cultivate and personalities to get to know. These include the new executive's boss, her peers, and perhaps (depending on the position) members of the board.

The newly hired executive needs to get to know each of these individuals as coworkers and as people. For each new colleague, she must answer many questions. How closely will the new executive need to work with this person? What are the peer's goals and aspirations for himself and for his group?

Usually there are one or two peers with whom a new executive will work closely. For a new vice president of product development, it might be the vice president of marketing and the vice president of operations. For a new vice president of marketing, it might be peers who lead product development and sales. They need to become allies, so cultivating collegial and collaborative relationships with them requires special focus and attention.

## Politics

In the context of business, the word *politics* has negative connotations. (Actually, this is true in just about every context, but that's another story.) People think of backstabbing or ingratiating colleagues, and an environment where success has more to do with playing political games than performance. It conjures an image of a workplace that feels like a medieval court, where you could find your head on the block for looking at someone the wrong way.

That's not what I'm talking about here. I'm referring to the dynamics of how members of an executive team work together. This is something every new executive needs to understand. Most people would agree, the organizational chart rarely reflects the actual intricacies of how power flows and decisions are made in a company.

Let's consider a hypothetical new executive. If she works for the CEO, she'll need to quickly understand his management and communications style.

She'll also need to get to know her peers on the management team. What are their interests? Are they aligned with those of the new executive, or in tension with them? Are there members of the management team who are held in especially high regard by the board or the CEO? Are there others who don't wield much influence, who have been relegated to the sidelines?

Then there are issues related directly to the new executive or her position. Is there someone who wanted the new executive's job and didn't get it? Is that person in a position to undermine her efforts? Are there peers who simply don't buy into the new executive's mission and are actively working against it? In both cases, these potential adversaries need to be identified and won over or, failing that, managed to the best degree possible.

There are other things it would be helpful to know, too. Is the CEO's brother-in-law the president of the company's largest division? Is his boyhood friend the CFO? Family and personal relationships create political cross-currents that are perilous to those who aren't aware of them.

## Culture

Just like people, companies have personalities. *Culture* is the shorthand term commonly used to describe the behavioral norms and values that characterize a company.

Some people think a company's culture doesn't matter. That's a big mistake. Executives who are insensitive to cultural norms find out the hard way that culture is as real as a brick wall.

Presumably the new executive has been hired, in part, because she is compatible with the company's culture. That's nice, but it doesn't mean she can walk in the door and immediately fit in. She has a lot of work to do to understand the intricacies of the company's culture and how to be effective within it.

Even language differs from company to company. For example, one of my clients, a CEO, told the marketing leader I recruited for him to "survey the field." He wanted the marketing head to discuss a new product idea with a few members of the field sales force. The new marketing person, however, came from a company where "survey the field" meant conducting a formal survey of the company's customers. They only discovered the misunderstanding after the marketing executive been working on the survey for several days.

## Setting Expectations

While the new executive is learning about the business, her department, and the company's people, politics, and culture, she's also assessing the current situation and formulating an action plan.

The objectives she defines become the benchmarks by which she will be measured. The short-term objectives—those that will be completed in the first few months—are particularly critical, because achieving them will establish her credibility, trustworthiness, and leadership. Conversely, failure to achieve them, or setting short-term objectives that others judge unimportant, puts the new executive on a path to failure. Her boss begins to doubt her ability to deliver, her peers start to suspect she is an unreliable ally, and her team questions her ability to lead.

## Onboarding: How to Do It

Let's say you buy my argument up to now. You see the steep learning curve that new executives must navigate, and the value to you and your company in helping them to integrate faster. That raises a new question: What's the best way to construct an onboarding program for new executive?

If your company has developed a formal onboarding program for new executives, it may solve your problem. However, these are exceedingly rare, and it's unlikely to be an option.

If your company does have a program in place, it's a sign that the company sees the value in onboarding, and that will help you. Involving your new executive in the program will be the path of least resistance, but make sure it is going to meet the needs of the new hire and you. It would be a mistake to assume that the program will provide what's needed, or that the individuals running it have the same self-interest in the new executive's success that the new executive and you do. By its very nature, onboarding a new executive must be highly customized. Every position and situation is unique, and a cookie-cutter approach won't work.

However, that's probably all hypothetical. The odds are overwhelming that there is no such program. Figuring out how to provide appropriate assistance to the new executive falls on your shoulders alone. That's not necessarily a bad thing, since you and the new executive are the ones with the most at stake, and therefore the most interest in doing a good job with his integration.

How can you attack this problem? There's not a simple answer because there are several options. Which one is best depends on the attitude of the individuals involved, the company context, and how much money you are willing to spend. Let's look at each of them.

## Do It All Yourself

The simplest option, and the cheapest, is for you coordinate all of the necessary onboarding activities. Indeed, you may be saying to yourself, "I already help my new executives to integrate into the company. I've got this handled."

Indeed, almost every manager takes a few basic steps to help new executives get rolling. But the emphasis should be on the word *few*, because usually the steps taken are grossly inadequate. Typically, the hiring manager sits down with the new executive on the first day to discuss whom he needs to meet within the company. They also discuss objectives, and perhaps schedule one or more visits to the field to meet key people at other offices or at business partners.

That's all great stuff, but the problem with these informal approaches to onboarding is that they tend to peter out very quickly. After the first couple of weeks, and certainly after the first month, the hiring manager backs off. She assumes that the new executive can proceed without help—and more often than not, the new executive makes the same assumption. This period, when everyone thinks the new executive knows more about the new environment than he really does, is when he is at the highest risk of running into trouble.

My suggestion is to put together an onboarding plan that feels informal but provides a solid structure that will keep everyone on track. At a minimum, it should provide for regular meetings with the new executive to discuss his integration for three to six months after his hire. Sticking to this discipline will help you both.

It will help the new executive because it sends him a message that integration is a long-term project. All too often, the new executive stops asking questions too early because he feels pressure to perform and is afraid that asking questions will make him look bad. Building an onboarding structure that extends months into his tenure gives him permission to keep asking questions, and to be open about the areas where he's struggling to come up to speed.

For the hiring manager, the meetings provide a constant reminder that the new executive is still learning, even well past the point when he's become a fixture in the office. Just creating that awareness makes the hiring manager much more likely to provide needed support, and less likely to have unrealistic expectations for performance.

Of course, to create the program, you need to build a list of everything the new executive needs to learn, and some kind of framework for learning it. Don't overthink. Early on—say, during the first two weeks—you may wish to direct the new executive's agenda. After that, however, he will naturally begin to direct his own learning. Be prepared to let him take over and to provide the support he needs.

## Get Help

What if you can't be involved to the extent I've just described? Perhaps your travel schedule takes you out of the office 80 percent of the time, or the new executive you've hired doesn't work at your location. Or maybe your plate is so full you know you'll never be able to give the new executive the attention he deserves. If you can't get it done alone, you need to get help.

You also need help if there's a history of turnover in the new executive's position, or if you've had more than your share of new executives fail early in their tenure. You need help figuring out what's going wrong so you don't suffer the same outcomes in the future.

One option is to hire an outside executive coach to assist with the new executive's onboarding. Coaching engagements for onboarding vary in length, but they typically last six months. The agreement will specify the goal of the assignment, a schedule of actions, and concrete deliverables such as reports on feedback, goal setting, and so on.

Part of what makes coaching relationships powerful is confidentiality. The coach is an outsider who promises that his interactions with the subject will remain private. The client can talk freely about her weaknesses, worries, family issues, or personality issues at work without fear of undermining herself or walking into a political minefield. Some bosses can be uncomfortable with this arrangement, but it simply doesn't work well when done any other way.

If you think hiring an onboarding coach makes sense, discuss the idea with the new hire. Ask him whether he likes the idea. Some will view the offer positively, as a sign that the company is willing to invest in their success. Others won't be interested in working with a coach. In the end, it has to be the executive's choice to participate. All the support in the world will be wasted if he doesn't want it.

Let's assume the new executive is willing to work with a coach and you can procure the funding. Identify several coaches (through your network, if possible) who have experience helping with executive transitions. You and the new hire should both interview them, but let the new hire make the final selection. The coaching relationship won't work unless the coach and the executive have good chemistry.

Executive coaches tell me that onboarding services are a very tough sell. After spending a lot of money to recruit a new executive, most companies have no appetite to spend even more to make the new executive successful. In some companies, even the suggestion of hiring a coach will be looked upon with scorn.

If you can't afford to hire a coach, or if it is simply impossible to do within your company's culture, there is another option. You can find an internal resource to help the new executive navigate his integration. Think of this as appointing an internal mentor, rather than hiring an outsider. It could be someone else from your staff, or an executive from a different part of the company.

Sometimes this approach is disparagingly referred to as "Just Follow Joe Around." I think that's unfair. While it's true that appointing an internal mentor will be very different from hiring an outside coach, it's still effective when it's taken seriously and the parties have good chemistry. An internal mentor can make a major contribution toward the new executive's early success.

### Here's What I Do

As an executive search consultant, I have a strong interest in the success of the people I recruit. I'm always confident that my client has chosen a capable candidate, but my hands-on involvement ends when the executive I've recruited starts work. That's always made me uncomfortable, because I know that onboarding (or rather, the lack of it) can be such an important factor in the new executive's success.

That's why I buy everyone I recruit a copy of *The First 90 Days*, the Michael Watkins book mentioned earlier in this chapter. It is a short, practical primer on how to successfully manage career transitions. I say to the new executive, "Most companies don't provide a lot of support to new executives. I don't know what kind of onboarding they have planned for you, or whether they will do anything at all. In any case, you need to take charge of your own transition. It's your job and your career. Read this book; it will help you devise a plan, and also help you avoid potentially fatal mistakes."

## Keep Your Star Players

One more important point. If you do everything suggested in this book, you'll be investing a significant effort in selecting and integrating the best possible employees for your team. The final piece of the puzzle is holding on to great talent once you have it.

A detailed discussion of retention strategy is beyond the scope of this book, but it is worth pointing out that you should have one. Too many companies spend freely on recruiting but do little to retain the great talent they already have. They don't have a plan for identifying key people and keeping them happy. The inevitable result is that, one after the other, the best people walk out the door.

In good times and bad, the best employees always have opportunities to leave. Executive recruiters, along with venture capitalists and others, are continually on the hunt for the best talent. We are calling them constantly, trying to lure them away with enticing new jobs.

Fortunately you can arm yourself against us. In fact, retention is not very complicated. You need a system to identify your best talent. Then you must make sure they are fairly compensated.

However, it's not all about money. The number-one reason stars change jobs is that they no longer see a path for career growth. They want to progress, but they feel like they are treading water. Great employees want to do interesting work, be challenged, improve their skills, and advance. You must have a deep understanding of your stars' goals, and use that to create plans to develop their careers within the company. Then you need to have a continuing dialogue about their career development and how you will help them get where they want to go.

Remember, if you don't help your stars advance and grow, someone like me will help them achieve their goals outside of your company.

## Summary

Selecting the right candidate is critically important, but it's only part of the battle. Most companies do nothing to help new executives integrate into the company and their jobs. As a result, many new executives who otherwise would have been successful fail early, or never achieve their potential.

- You will improve the success rate of new hires if you take an active role in helping them learn about the company, the job, and the culture.
- Help the new executive set and achieve short-term objectives that will demonstrate her competence and win trust and respect from her colleagues and subordinates.
- If you can't do everything yourself, get some help from someone who's willing to be an internal mentor or from an outside consultant.
- There will be bumps in the road. Help the new executive avoid unwitting missteps. Despite those efforts, you can count on any new hire making mistakes anyway. Be there to help him recover when it happens.
- Don't let the onboarding process fizzle out too early. Put together a plan that extends for at least six months. Of course, the intensity of the effort will taper over time, but it shouldn't end prematurely. It takes a new executive up to a year to get up to speed.
- Most companies neglect their best performers and suffer unnecessary turnover as a result. Don't forget about retention, or you will find yourself recruiting new executives far more often than necessary.

## Notes

1. Michael D. Watkins, *The First Ninety Days* (Boston: Harvard Business Review Press, 2013). Watkins introduces the idea on page 1, but it's the topic of the entire book.

2. Joseph Daniel McCool, *Deciding Who Leads: How Executive Recruiters Drive, Direct, and Disrupt the Global Search for Management Talent* (Mountain View: Davies-Black, 2008), 109.

3. Bradford D. Smart, *Topgrading: How Leading Companies Win by Hiring, Coaching, and Keeping the Best People* (New York: Penguin Group, 2005), 46.

4. McCool, *Deciding Who Leads*, 124–125.

# Chapter 10

# The Path to Mastery

One reason so many people feel uncomfortable with recruiting is that they don't gather enough information through interviews and references, and consequently they feel like they're making decisions in the dark. More often than not, they are.

You won't have that problem if you follow the game plan laid out in this book. It will force you to gather as much information as possible about job candidates. Armed with data, you will make better recruiting decisions right away.

That doesn't mean the decisions will be easy. In the beginning, it's likely you'll make decisions slowly, and frequently second-guess yourself. That's part of the learning process. Speed and confidence will come with experience and, eventually, mastery.

## Portrait of a Master

In the first chapter of this book, I noted that executives who excel at recruiting have a set of skills that can appear mysterious to those who don't have them. What is it that enables them to make consistently high-quality decisions when evaluating people?

### Eric

Let's start with a profile of a recruiting master I'll call Eric. Eric is the CEO of a medium-sized public company that is a leader in its market. The company's success is largely attributable to Eric's leadership, and particularly to the high-quality people that he has succeeded in recruiting and retaining over the years. His recruiting track record is far above average, and an overwhelming majority of his hires go on to have long and successful careers with the company. By the ultimate measure—overall financial performance—the company beats its peers by a considerable margin.

For an executive recruiter like me, Eric is an ideal client because he knows what he wants, makes decisions quickly, and doesn't vacillate. When we begin a search, he has already developed clear and detailed thoughts on the specifics of the job to be filled and the experience that he seeks in candidates.

What makes Eric a master, however, is his ability to expertly assess how well candidates will fit within his company and its culture. To put it simply, he's great at judging fit.

There are three reasons Eric is so good at this. First, he knows what he's looking for—he knows exactly what personal traits candidates must have to be successful in his organization. If you ask him what defines his company's culture, he will give you a crisp and clear answer. Because he can articulate what makes his company culture unique, he has a well-defined yardstick against which to measure the candidates he's evaluating.

The second reason Eric is so good at gauging fit is because he is an outstanding judge of people. He can confidently assess intangible traits and behaviors like personality, motivation, intelligence, social skills, and the ability to work well with others. His ability to judge people is highly intuitive, and he can make rapid decisions. For example, he will immediately eliminate a candidate from contention if he believes she is a poor fit for the organization.

Third, while Eric is quick to make a negative judgment of candidates, he is slow to make an affirmative one. He never rushes to make a hire, because he knows that the risks of making a bad decision in haste are too high. He keeps an open mind and never short-circuits the hiring process or forces his choice on the rest of his team.

Candidates tell me Eric is a tough interview. He asks challenging questions that probe accomplishments, problem solving, teamwork, and raw intelligence. He treats everyone well but keeps a professional distance. In fact, more than a few candidates have told me, "That guy's hard to read." When Eric provides feedback to me on candidates, he always has thoughtful insights.

When a candidate makes it through a first meeting with Eric, he advances to a series of interviews with other key people who will be involved in the hire. These interviews are no formality: Eric puts a very high value on the opinions of his key lieutenants, and a poor review from any of them can sink a candidacy.

When it's time to do references, Eric will always pick up the phone and call a couple of them himself, usually the candidate's last two managers. He focuses not only on validating the candidate's potential but also on learning how he can manage her most effectively if she comes on board.

Eric's adherence to process, the weight he gives to the opinions of his team, and his reluctance to rush to decisions come from awareness that his judgment, as good as it is, is still imperfect. His healthy self-confidence is tempered with a useful dose of humility. He is painfully aware that he can make mistakes—because he has made them in the past. In fact, if you ask him how he got so good at recruiting, he will tell you it was a difficult process, and that he made some poor decisions along the way.

## Suzanne

Suzanne is the CEO of a young, high-growth company that is in the early stages of commercializing its first product. Because the company is new, its culture is a blank slate. Suzanne knows that one of her most important jobs is to create a culture that will enable the company to thrive.

Suzanne's personality is nothing like Eric's, but their approach to recruiting is quite similar. Like Eric, she goes into a search with a crystal-clear vision of what she wants. She makes the search a priority, and reviews resumes and interviews candidates promptly. She's decisive, and she takes the input from other team members seriously. She follows a rigorous process.

Suzanne is an outstanding judge of people, and usually knows after the first meeting whether a candidate will fit into the culture she is building. She looks for people with high energy, outstanding social skills, intelligence, and a passion to help build something new and exciting. Her feel for people is highly intuitive.

In contrast with Eric, who prefers to handle executive searches without the assistance of his HR group, Suzanne always involves the company's HR leader. She values the HR leader's advice—and also relies on her to make sure that interviews are scheduled promptly and that I get feedback in a timely way.

Like Eric, Suzanne knows she's not perfect. In fact, she actively seeks advice from trusted mentors, who provide guidance on the myriad challenges that CEOs face. I've never met a CEO so committed to self-examination and self-improvement.

## Mark

Mark is quite different from Suzanne and Eric. He's a serial entrepreneur with a creative intellect that moves from idea to idea like wildfire. Over the years he's built several successful companies in multiple industries.

Mark is one of the more open and self-aware people I've ever met. He knows his strengths and weaknesses, and he won't hesitate to tell you what they are. He places a very high value on operational rigor, but it's neither his forte nor his interest. He surrounds himself with competent lieutenants who free him to focus on the big picture. A strong CFO handles finance, an operational guru handles manufacturing, and he hires me to handle executive-level recruiting.

Mark is an incredibly intuitive and insightful judge of people. In interviews, he combines compelling salesmanship with challenging and probing questions. He comes away from those meetings with a strong sense of the candidate's skills and character.

Like Suzanne and Eric, Mark won't make rash hiring decisions. He knows that the stakes are far too high. He carefully weighs input from his staff and trusted board members, and looks to referencing to validate his assessment of the candidate.

## Expertise Explained

It's likely that you know at least one person like Eric, Suzanne, or Mark, who has mastered the art of recruiting. Most of us know masters when we see them, but we have a hard time defining exactly what makes them so effective. What is it, and how did they get that way?

I believe that mastery consists of a constellation of synergistic skills and behaviors. They reinforce each other, and together they create the ability to make good decisions with confidence and relative speed. When someone has achieved mastery, the process of recruiting has become second nature.

The defining characteristic of recruiting masters is that they are outstanding judges of people. This ability has been acquired over time through focused repetition. A master has made dozens of hiring decisions (mostly good, some bad), and the sum of those experiences has refined her ability to assess candidates. The pinnacle of mastery is the ability to make a highly accurate decision about a candidate's suitability in a rapid, almost unconscious way. This skill looks mysterious, but it's the residue of expertise that's been earned through hard work and years of experience.

That's good news for everyone who wants to get better at recruiting, because it means that assessing people is a learnable skill. To be sure, beginners will start at different levels. Some might have a head start if they begin the learning process with high self-confidence or outstanding interpersonal abilities. Those traits alone, however, aren't sufficient without hard work to develop the other qualities that make up expertise. And, conversely, those who are not naturals are perfectly capable of achieving mastery. No matter your level today, you can become expert if you work hard.

Masters of recruiting also share a set of attitudes that, taken together, create a foundation that supports and enables their recruiting skill. These include humility, willingness to listen, maturity, and an affinity for people. I use the word *attitudes* because I don't believe these are immutable elements of character. Rather, I believe they are behaviors that these people have learned over time, through work and life experience.

Let's look at these attitudes in detail.

Recruiting masters, like all effective business leaders, have self-confidence that's well above average, but they remain keenly aware of their ability to make mistakes. As a result, they build in safeguards that protect them from making bad hires. They avoid quick decisions, stick to the discipline of a sound recruiting process, and solicit the opinions of trusted colleagues.

They also listen to input from others, especially when it contradicts their own thinking. In other words, they keep an open mind. They're always testing their own opinions against those of smart, strong-minded colleagues.

Another attitude they share is maturity. Maturity can mean a lot of things, but in this context I mean holding a realistic view of one's own strengths and weaknesses, and being at peace with them. Another way to put it is the commonplace expression, "to be comfortable in one's own skin."

Executives who lack maturity bring psychological baggage to the process of hiring. Recruiting can be highly stressful, and it can bring out an immature executive's worst fears and insecurities. When that happens, it becomes very difficult to make sound decisions. Mature executives don't have this problem. They have an easier time staying calm and grounded, and make decisions without the interference of strong emotions.

Finally, masters of recruiting enjoy interacting with other people and have excellent interpersonal skills. That doesn't mean they have to be extroverts, but it does mean they cannot be misanthropes, or so deeply introverted that they avoid interactions with others.

It's worth restating that masters and beginners alike must follow the same process. Expertise is defined, in part, by the ability to execute the process with great skill. To restate an example from earlier in the book, consider the great cellist Yo-Yo Ma. He doesn't get to take liberties with the notes in a piece of music. He is an expert precisely because he can play those notes with fluidity and insight. In the same way, those who have mastered recruiting still must follow the process, but they can execute it with great confidence and speed, and achieve desired outcomes.

## Building Your Plan

How can you get on the path to mastery? It won't happen overnight, but this book provides a framework that you can use, no matter your current skill level, to become better at executive-level hiring. Becoming an expert is a long-term project, but the quality of your hires will improve immediately if you follow the process laid out in this book. If you follow this book's program over the long haul, you will achieve mastery much faster than if you took a more haphazard and less disciplined approach.

Here's a simple, five-step approach that will help you to make better hires right now—and, over time, to achieve the mastery of recruiting.

### Step One: Commitment

The first step is making a commitment. Hiring great people is difficult and requires a lot of time and effort. If you're serious about improving, it will take hard work. It's no different from acquiring any other skill. If you want to learn to play a musical instrument, you must practice every day. If you want to learn to play tennis, you must spend a lot of time on the court. If you want to get better at recruiting, you must make a commitment to doing it in a thoughtful way.

## FIVE STEPS TO MASTERY

1 COMMITMENT

2 SELF ASSESSMENT

3 GET A MENTOR

4 FOLLOW THE PLAN

5 REGULARLY TAKE STOCK OF PROGRESS

Many people never get better at recruiting because short-term issues constantly distract them. It's understandable: when you're fighting difficult short-term problems, it's easy to push recruiting to the bottom of your to-do list.

Don't allow that to happen. If you believe that your most important task is building a great team, then you must give it the attention it requires and deserves. It takes discipline to stay focused on recruiting when dozens of other pressing matters are vying for your attention. The ability to look past today's problems and give sustained attention to long-term projects like recruiting is one of the characteristics that separate good executives from ineffectual ones.

Now let's look at the concrete steps you can take to build and execute your plan.

## Step Two: Self-Assessment

Before developing an action plan, take stock of your skill level and track record. How much experience do you have recruiting executives? Have your recruits been successful, or have they failed to live up to expectations?

Self-assessment will enable you to identify areas that need attention. It will also benchmark your past performance, at least in an informal way, so you can measure your progress over time.

Use the following list to guide your review. Be honest with yourself. It can be difficult to take a critical look at your own performance, but it's a necessary step toward self-improvement in recruiting (and everything else in life).

Write down your answers to these questions and file them away for future reference. You'll want to look at them later to assess your progress. Based on your answers, you'll be able to place yourself into one of three categories: *apprentice, journeyman,* or *artisan.*

If you've done little to no executive-level recruiting, you're an *apprentice.* You're just beginning to learn the craft. Although you don't have much experience, this is a good place to be. You haven't acquired any bad habits, and you haven't made recruiting mistakes that might cause your boss and peers to question your abilities or judgment. Further, the fact that you are reading this book means you are motivated to learn. All of these things create a strong foundation for rapid progress and long-term success.

If you have some experience hiring executives, but not enough to have mastered the process or to see the results you desire, you're a *journeyman.*

## SELF ASSESSMENT QUESTIONS

》 How many executive level hires have you made in the past?

》 How many of your hires have been outstanding? Good but not great? Outright mistakes?

》 Which parts of the hiring process, if any, have you mastered?

》 Which parts do you find difficult or make you uneasy?

》 Rate your own performance in the following areas:

  • Building a clear definition of the position and the ideal candidate

  • Building consensus with other key people on the new hire

  • Partnering with HR or outside recruiters

  • Promptly dealing with recruiting matters, such as evaluating resumes, scheduling interviews, and so on.

  • Selling the company and the position to candidates

  • Interviewing

  • Treating candidates with respect

  • Referencing (or directing the referencing work of others)

  • Drafting of the job offer

  • Presenting the job offer

  • Supporting integration of the new hire into the company

》 Do you have a mentor who provides advice on recruiting?

You have a strong foundation but need more focused practice to build expertise. If you have made mistakes along the way, you also may have some bad habits that need to be unlearned. You are well positioned to continue building your skills.

If you've already achieved mastery, you're an *artisan*. You've built an outstanding track record, and the executives you recruit have a high rate of success. Years of experience have made you very comfortable with the recruiting process, and you can execute it with fluidity. You've developed the ability to assess candidates quickly and accurately. Your peers say you are a great judge of people. You don't need this book, but it may be a helpful tool for people on your staff.

## Step Three: Get Help

Before you begin this journey, you need a trusted colleague who can serve as a sounding board. This person could be a peer, a mentor, a coach, an HR leader at your company, or someone else. It doesn't matter what you call the relationship or how you formalize it, as long as you find someone who is willing and able to provide the help you need.

Self-study (through books like this one, for example) is an excellent way to learn, but your progress will be much faster if you have a colleague from whom you can solicit criticism and advice. Think about it: you can learn to swing a golf club from a book, but you will learn much faster if a real person is helping you. The same holds true for recruiting. All of us have blind spots, behaviors that are invisible to us but obvious to others. A trusted colleague will hold up a mirror so you can see yourself more clearly, or provide a push to get you back on track.

Find someone you respect and trust. It's essential that this be a person with whom you are willing to share your struggles. If you're unwilling to talk about the areas in which you're experiencing difficulties, you won't get anything out of the relationship. Further, you must be willing to listen. Why bother soliciting advice from a trusted friend or colleague if you are not open to hearing constructive criticism or changing your own behavior?

It doesn't matter how many years of experience you have or your level of expertise. In fact, many CEOs of Fortune 100 companies employ coaches. If you want to improve as quickly as possible and perform at your best, get a mentor.

## Step Four: Execution

To get going, use this book as your instruction manual. If you follow the roadmap found here, you will learn to do things the right way, and your odds of success will be high.

If you're an *apprentice*, the first few searches you conduct will require particularly intensive work as you learn the process. Further, it's likely you will feel unsure of yourself as you make your first hiring decisions. Don't be discouraged; this is a natural consequence of learning something new. The good news is you will be on a very steep learning curve, and after a few recruiting projects the process will begin to feel familiar and comfortable as you make it your own.

If you're a *journeyman*, you'll be honing your skills. If you need to shed bad habits, unlearning them can be a challenge. If you simply follow the guidelines in this book (and don't slide back into the old way of doing things), you'll make progress toward correcting whatever problems are holding down your rate of success. It can be quite difficult to adopt a new set of behaviors when other ones have become ingrained—just ask anyone who's trying to stick to a new diet—but if you do so, a much higher percentage of your new executive hires will be successful.

Regardless of where you start, over time you will develop expertise, and that will enable you to make decisions more quickly and with more confidence. You'll get a better intuitive feel for each candidate's personality and how they might fit (or not fit) into your organization.

### Step Five: Regularly Reassess

Every six to twelve months (or whenever you feel like you've hit a roadblock), review your progress. Pull your answers to the self-assessment questions out of your files and review where you started. Have you made progress?

If you're sticking to your plan, the odds are that you are improving, and your answers to the self-assessment questions will remind you how far you've come. I've kept notebooks to record my performance in the gym for many years for the same reason. When I'm feeling discouraged, I review my past performance and am almost always surprised to find I am doing better than I thought.

If you believe you are following the plan but aren't seeing results, you need help figuring out what's going wrong. Sit down with your mentor or a trusted colleague and try to understand what's happening. It's likely that you have a blind spot, and counsel from a third party is the best and fastest way to figure out what it is.

Of course, if you're not sticking to your plan, you'll find you haven't made progress. If so, don't waste time beating yourself up. Instead, use your energy in a constructive way by making a renewed commitment to the project, and resolving to bring new energy and discipline to your recruiting efforts.

### Staying Motivated

Mastering recruiting doesn't happen overnight. Mastery (not only of recruiting but of anything) is a long-term goal that will take many years to achieve. It's easy to get discouraged when the ultimate objective is very far away.

You can avoid the discouragement trap by focusing on short-term goals. For example, you can't reasonably expect to become an expert after one year. If you measure yourself against that goalpost, especially when you're just starting out, you are liable to become disheartened. Instead, focus on things you can achieve in the near-term. In the first year, for example, you can certainly implement a more disciplined recruiting process and make a larger percentage of successful hires than you have in the past. That would be an outstanding outcome.

Focus on those small, incremental improvements. When you're discouraged because you're still uncomfortable recruiting, or you regret a recent decision, remind yourself how far you have come. It's important to savor the small victories and enjoy the process. To be sure, you will make mistakes. When that happens, analyze what went wrong, learn from the experience, and then let it go.

Finally, remember that perfection is not attainable. If you expect to achieve a perfect hiring record you will be bitterly disappointed, even if your performance is outstanding. Recruiting is like hitting a baseball—success is measured in percentages. A hitter who bats .400—that is, gets a hit four times out of ten—is extraordinary. An executive who excels at recruiting will do considerably better than that—maybe eight out of ten—but he will never be perfect. Celebrate the small improvements in the success rate of your hires, because they are a significant achievement that has high value for your business.

## Final Thoughts

The premise of this book is that only a human being with hard-earned expertise can assess candidates for executive-level jobs. This isn't a controversial idea; business leaders take it as a given. They know there aren't any shortcuts through the thicket of human behavior that makes recruiting executives so difficult.

As I write these words, there is a growing movement to apply computer screening to the assessment and selection of job candidates. While there are situations where this technology is useful, I fear it is being grossly misused. Computers eliminate candidates from consideration before a human ever views their resumes, and tests of dubious validity recommend candidates for hire. The tail is wagging the proverbial dog.

For now, the use of technology is focused on low- and mid-level jobs, but it's only a matter of time before we see claims that assessment of executives can be quantified, too. When that happens, be deeply skeptical.

You wouldn't let a computer choose your spouse or your friends. Why would you let it decide whom you should hire?

Recruiting at the executive level is and will remain the sole province of human experts. There's something uniquely complex about human beings and our social interactions. We are not biological robots that can be described by a set of equations and then fit into the perfect job by a computer. People are far more than that, and that's why recruiting executives is fascinating, exhilarating, and exasperating all at the same time.

I wish you the best as you master the art of recruiting. I hope you find the journey as interesting and rewarding as I have.

# Index

## About the Author

**MICHAEL TRAVIS,** named by *BusinessWeek* as one of the World's Most Influential Headhunters, is the principal of Travis & Company, an executive search firm. For almost two decades, Travis has served clients by recruiting general management, function heads, and board directors. His clients range in size from raw startups to *Fortune* 50 companies.

Travis has worked with hundreds of hiring managers. He's seen the full spectrum of ability, from those rare CEOs who have mastered hiring to those who need remedial help. His broad experience has given him a unique perspective on where hiring managers make mistakes and how they can improve their performance. Travis observes that most hiring managers have been poorly prepared for recruiting and are hungry for practical advice on how to get better.

Travis is frequently approached by the media to offer commentary on topics related to executive search, with recent coverage in the *Boston Business Journal, The New York Times, Executive Recruiter News,* and other business publications. He also writes a blog on executive hiring (www.travisandco.com/blog).